JEWISH ENCOUNTERS

Jonathan Rosen, General Editor

Jewish Encounters is a collaboration between Schocken and Nextbook, a project devoted to the promotion of Jewish literature, culture, and ideas.

D0368365

>nextbook

PUBLISHED

THE LIFE OF DAVID · Robert Pinsky
MAIMONIDES · Sherwin B. Nuland
BARNEY ROSS · Douglas Century
BETRAYING SPINOZA · Rebecca Goldstein
EMMA LAZARUS · Esther Schor
THE WICKED SON · David Mamet
MARC CHAGALL · Jonathan Wilson
JEWS AND POWER · Ruth R. Wisse
BENJAMIN DISRAELI · Adam Kirsch
RESURRECTING HEBREW · Ilan Stavans
THE JEWISH BODY · Melvin Konner
A FINE ROMANCE · David Lehman
RASHI · Elie Wiesel

FORTHCOMING

THE CAIRO GENIZA · Adina Hoffman and Peter Cole
THE WORLD OF SHOLOM ALEICHEM · Jeremy Dauber
MOSES · Stephen J. Dubner
BIROBIJAN · Masha Gessen
JUDAH MACCABEE · Jeffrey Goldberg
YEHUDA HA'LEVI · Hillel Halkin
NACHMAN/KAFKA · Rodger Kamenetz
THE DAIRY RESTAURANT · Ben Katchor
THE SONG OF SONGS · Elena Lappin
ABRAHAM CAHAN · Seth Lipsky
THE EICHMANN TRIAL · Deborah Lipstadt
SHOW OF SHOWS · David Margolick
JEWS AND MONEY · Daphne Merkin
WHEN GRANT EXPELLED THE JEWS · Jonathan Sarna
HILLEL · Joseph Telushkin
MESSIANISM · Leon Wieseltier

Barney Ross

DOUGLAS CENTURY

BARNEY ROSS

The Life of a Jewish Fighter

NEXTBOOK · SCHOCKEN · NEW YORK

Schocken Books and colophon are registered trademarks of
Random House, Inc.

Originally published in hardcover in the United States by
Schocken Books, a division of Random House, Inc.,
New York, in 2006.

Unless otherwise noted, all photographs are courtesy of
George Rasof.

Library of Congress Cataloging-in-Publication Data
Century, Douglas.
    Barney Ross / Douglas Century.
        p. cm. — (Jewish encounters)
    Includes bibliographical references.
    ISBN 978-0-8052-1173-3
    1. Ross, Barney. 2. Boxers (Sports)—United States—
Biography. 3. Jewish boxers—United States—Biography.
I. Title. II. Series.
GV1132.R65C46 2006   796.83'092—dc22   [B]   2005049939

www.schocken.com

Printed in the United States of America
First Paperback Edition
2 4 6 8 9 7 5 3 1

FOR MY DAUGHTER

Lena Juliet Century

AND IN LOVING MEMORY OF

MY BOXING-LOVING CHICAGO UNCLES

Abe Levy

(1910–2002)

Roy Smith

(1934–1983)

עליהם השלום

For a while during my adolescence I studiously followed prizefighting, could recite the names and weights of all the champions and contenders. . . . From my father and his friends I heard about the prowess of Benny Leonard, Barney Ross, Max Baer and the colorfully named Slapsie Maxie Rosenbloom. . . . In my scheme of things, Slapsie Maxie was a more remarkable Jewish phenomenon by far than Dr. Albert Einstein.

—PHILIP ROTH, *The Facts*

CONTENTS

INTRODUCTION

Life was a never-ending battle for Barney Ross. Though he is still widely regarded as one of the two greatest Jewish boxers of the twentieth century—forever linked to his immediate forebear, the long-reigning lightweight champion Benny Leonard—he sprang from a tradition that placed little value on the art of self-defense. Indeed, throughout his adult life Ross often told the story of a pogrom his father had witnessed as a young man, a tale illustrative of his ultra-Orthodox family's abhorrence of any sort of physical violence. The prizefighter's father, Reb Yitchak (Itchik) Rasofsky, was a Talmudic scholar and Hebrew teacher in Brest-Litovsk, then a thriving center for Jewish commerce, culture, and scholarship on the border between Belorussia and Poland. A lean, red-bearded man about five feet nine, his perfect posture, Barney remembered, made him seem "erect like a soldier." Reb Itchik was praying one afternoon in a small Brest-Litovsk synagogue when a mob stormed inside chanting "Death to the Jews." They smashed windows, broke the mahogany door of the ark, and desecrated the holy Torah scrolls. Reb Itchik was struck by a stone, knocked to the ground, and surrounded by men hissing "*Zhid*." Like the other terrified Jews, he did not fight back.

In later years, whenever Barney's father remembered that

pogrom, he would point to the close-clipped hair at his temples and his curling sidelocks, which overnight, he said, had gone from auburn to white. By the time Barney was old enough to understand his father's meaning, old enough to comprehend that Jews could be hated simply for being born Jews, he was a scrappy, undernourished ten-year-old growing up surrounded by violence in the Maxwell Street ghetto on Chicago's Near West Side. To his young American ears, his father's lectures seemed as unfathomable and foreign as the caftan-clad greenhorns still flooding by the thousands into the Maxwell Street tenements. It was drummed into the five Rasofsky sons again and again: a devout Jew should never raise his fists—even in self-defense. "The religious man," Barney recalled his father saying, "prizes learning above everything else. Let the atheists be the fighters, the *trumbeniks*, the murderers—we are the scholars."

Beryl Rasofsky—celebrated in his twenties as the world's lightweight, junior-welterweight, and welterweight champion, decorated in his thirties for his "conspicuous gallantry" in the Battle of Guadalcanal—never lived by his father's credo. He became a street tough—a *trumbenik*—went clean-shaven, wore hand-tailored three-piece suits, camel-hair coats, snap-brim fedoras in shades from robin's-egg blue to charcoal grey. He tattooed his own initials on his forearm—in defiance of the Mosaic law*—chain-smoked and drank heavily, rubbed shoulders with bootleggers and bookmakers, and married a *Ziegfeld Follies* showgirl. He

*From Deuteronomy 14:1: "Ye are the children of the LORD your God: ye shall not cut yourselves. . . ."

made, then quickly squandered, his fighting fortune, estimated at half a million Depression-era dollars, earned boxing in prize rings after sunset on the Sabbath, when his father—had he lived long enough—would not have even switched on the Philco to listen.

I first heard the legend of Barney Ross when I was around ten years old. It was the mid-seventies, and I was a student at a small Yiddish elementary school in the foothills of the Canadian Rocky Mountains, founded by Yiddish-speaking socialists and dedicated to the memory of the towering modernist short-story writer I. L. Peretz. We were far too young, of course, to realize how incongruous it was, too young to know that we were the last of a breed—the final generation of Jews to be educated in the language and the old secular ways of the Yiddish socialists, that ours was a tradition, as fading, in its own way, as that of the proudly painted and feathered Blackfoot braves we saw in their annual midsummer powwow at the Calgary Exhibition and Stampede.

We spent our Peretz *shul* lunch hours chasing each other across the little gravel and dead-grass playground, consumed with daydreams of Jewish warriors, pretending we could lead a rebellion like Bar Kochba or Judah Maccabee, or camp beneath the moonlight as our principal had once done with the partisans. *Lehrer* Eichler—we always addressed him by the Yiddish honorific—was a small, broad-chested, fierce-eyed man who'd been born near the city of L'vov, or

Lemberg, in Poland. He had escaped from a Nazi *Arbeitslager* when he was only nine; an uncle had instructed him to slip on his two pairs of pants on the morning of the mass escape through the wire. He told us he had glimpsed his uncle machine-gunned to death as they fled, pushing him and others forward with the words, "Run, children, run!" Before long, he and his younger brother found themselves living among a ragged band of Jewish fighters in the forest, hardened little soldiers. Most of us regarded him with a mixture of terror and awe, particularly on Yom Ha-Shoah, or on the anniversary of the Warsaw ghetto uprising, when he would hold up those thick hands stamped with the hieroglyphics of forest survival: a finger that had been caught in the belt of a partisan's machine gun, another gashed from a bayonet, another nicked by a German bullet . . .

He coached our soccer games, occasionally exhibiting a few skillful flicks with his shiny dress shoes; he also loved to talk about the rich history of Jewish athletics. One morning I recall our *lehrer* telling me about the champion boxer and World War II hero Barney Ross. He had once met Ross, then late in life, when the white-haired boxer was traveling through western Canada on a fund-raising tour for State of Israel Bonds. Several photos of the silver-haired prizefighter still exist somewhere in the archives of the Jewish Historical Society of Southern Alberta. More than any other Jewish athlete—more than my Chicago-born father's beloved Sid Luckman, the prototype of the T-formation quarterback, more than Sandy Koufax or Mark Spitz—the legend of this sinewy prizefighter who'd danced into the ring in a tattered

Barney Ross, "The Pride of the Ghetto,"
in his championship years.

blue-and-white terrycloth bathrobe, billed as "The Pride of
the Ghetto," transfixed me.

I promptly looked him up in the school's edition of the
Encyclopedia Judaica, then attempted to sketch his likeness on
foolscap, showing his slicked-back hair as shiny as his Ever-
last shorts, his stare as passionate as any sword-wielding
Zealot. I remember sitting cross-legged on the library floor,
gnawing on my pencil, reading how Barney Ross had conquered the world as a prizefighter; how he'd joined the
Marines and become one of America's national heroes in the
bloody fighting in the jungle-covered South Pacific hell of

Guadalcanal. I learned too—and this to me had the most terrible resonance, like something out of the imagination of Dickens, or Peretz, for that matter—that as a boy of thirteen he had witnessed his father gunned down during a botched holdup. His mother collapsed with a nervous breakdown, and the family was shattered, Barney's younger brothers and sister sent off to an orphanage. Barney, the third child of six, vowed to make enough money to reunite the family, and fighting with his fists was the only way he knew how to do it.

I read that in Ross's boxing prime he'd been seen by Jews around the world as a living embodiment of what Max Nordau had spoken of in 1898 at the Second Zionist Congress in Basel in his call for a *Muskeljudentum*, that new philosophy which summoned the "sons of the Maccabees to rise again," exhorting a young generation to "train not only your spirit but your muscles as well."

But as I grew older, living now in New York, and began to actively search out the long-buried details of his biography—and was fortunate enough to get to know his surviving brother, nephew, and cousins—I found myself staring into the dark well of a largely inscrutable life; a life well documented by newsmen of his day, yet now largely unremembered except among boxing aficionados; a life shot through with half-truths and mysteries, but also a life that seemed uncannily mythic. Had Barney Ross really worked as a teenage message boy for Al Capone? Had he, in his late thirties, tried to run guns to the Zionist fighters during the State of Israel's War of Independence? Ross had an almost Zelig-like relationship to the major events of his day—the rise of Nazism, the birth of the modern sports celebrity, Zionism, drug addiction and recovery. He embodied the fantasy of Jewish force and was, at the same time, a cautionary tale against the physical life. He became an emblematic Jew only by stepping outside of his Orthodox upbringing and into the boxing ring—but he brought his Jewish identity with him in often unexpected ways.

It didn't take long to discern the intense vulnerability behind the warrior's mask; a "muscular Jew" he may have appeared to the outside world, and yet, on some profound level, Barney Ross had the fragility of an orchid. Some contemporary press accounts described him as "the gentle champion," owing to the fact that he lacked the brutal finishing instinct thought to be a prerequisite in his profession. I've been told by people who watched him train for his big fights that he sometimes stopped to apologize to his sparring partners if he hurt them. The late sports columnist Milton Gross, who knew the boxer well, summed up the knot of contradictions of the little boxer: "If prodigality was his nature, laughter was his signature. He was soft-spoken and happy-go-lucky outside the ring, but inside it he was a furious machine, completely devoid of fear."

Barney Ross

PART ONE

1

Barney Ross was a *kohain*, born into the ancient priestly caste, and reared by his father to become not a pugilist but a Hebrew teacher and Talmudic scholar. Indeed, the Rasofskys were directly related to Rabbi Baruch Leib Rosowsky, famed cantor of the Great Synagogue of Gogol Street in Vilna. By Jewish tradition, *kohanim* are said to be descendants of the High Priest Aaron, forbidden by religious law to visit cemeteries or have contact with anything impure; on Rosh Hashanah and Yom Kippur, Barney and his older brothers would walk up to the front of the synagogue, remove their shoes without touching the laces, wrap themselves in their *talaysim*, extend their hands, and confer the priestly blessing, the *birchas kohanim*, on the congregation.

In Brest-Litovsk, in addition to his virtually unpaid work as a Hebrew teacher, Reb Itchik had worked as a dairyman and small grocer, traveling the surrounding towns by oxcart. Following the state-sanctioned 1903 pogroms, most horrifically in the city of Kishinev—"City of Slaughter," in the words of the Hebrew poet Chaim Nachman Bialik-Rasofsky—Itchik saved up enough to make the passage to New York, leaving behind his wife, Sarah, and their firstborn son, Ben, with a promise that he would earn enough money to bring them later.

Itchik arrived on the Lower East Side in November 1903, his name now anglicized to Isidore, and, finding that the crowded Jewish ghetto had more than its share of Hebrew teachers, went to work selling a variety of vegetables, butter, and eggs from a pushcart. He graduated to a horse and wagon, and working tirelessly—sometimes one hundred hours a week, Barney later said—it took him two years to save enough money to bring over his wife and son, now nine, from Russia, where they settled in a dingy basement apartment on Rivington Street.

Sarah Rasofsky—née Epstein—was a small, soft-featured woman from the Polish town of Selz. In her later years she would become heavyset and frail, nearly blind from diabetes and glaucoma, but in her twenties she had the strength to go to work alongside her husband on the grocery wagon. It was hardly the *goldeneh medina* they had imagined; they fell into the venal Lower East Side tumult novelist Michael Gold gives us in *Jews Without Money:* "Pimps, gamblers and red-nosed bums; peanut politicians, pugilists in sweaters; tin-horn sports and tall longshoremen in overalls." The family was never far from starvation and illness; two children, indeed, died in infancy. Then Sarah gave birth to a second son, named Morrie.

Her third son arrived on December 23, 1909. He was named Dov-Ber, a distinctively Ashkenazic doubling of the Hebrew and Yiddish words for "bear." His school records list him as "Barnet David Rasofsky," his United States

Marine Corps discharge papers have it "Barney David Ross," but among family and close friends he was generally known by one of three affectionate Yiddish nicknames: Beryl, Beryleh, or Berchik—variants of "Little Bear."

Before he was two years old, the family, barely subsisting in New York, set out by train for Chicago, where Sarah's uncle Sam Rosenberg had a small grocery store for sale in the Maxwell Street ghetto. They arrived in 1911 and settled on Jefferson Street, in the hub of an outdoor market that sociologist Louis Wirth described as "full of color, action, shouts, odors, and dirt . . . resembl[ing] a medieval European fair more than the market of a great city today. Its origins are to be sought in the traditions of the Jews, whose occupations in the Old World differed little from what they are here."

In the crowded tenements, outbreaks of tuberculosis, pneumonia, and cholera were endemic. The Rasofskys' two-room apartment would soon grow more crowded with the arrival in just a few-year span of three more children— daughter Ida, and sons Sam and George. But rarely were they all in the apartment together; Sarah and Itchik worked such long hours that their sons remembered them practically living inside their store.

Some accounts have listed the establishment, at 1307 South Jefferson, as "Rasofsky's Dairy," but in fact it was so ramshackle that it had no name. Nor was there room for three customers to stand at one time amid the bags of flour and canned goods and pickle barrels. The Rasofskys lived directly across the street at number 1310 South Jefferson, and from their second-floor apartment window, above a bakery, Barney and his brothers could watch their father in his apron and skullcap, and on days when there was a flood of customers, Sarah or one of the boys would be constantly dashing across the street to help. In lieu of a cash register, Itchik and Sarah wrote all the transactions in pencil, and on the wall, tacked in place, regular customers would leave their credit tabs scrawled on scraps of paper bag. Sunday being the busy market day on Maxwell Street, the entire family would be enlisted in the bustling business—Barney and Morrie lifting heavy sacks, Ida taking customers' orders, Sammy and Georgie selling cherry phosphates on the sidewalk for two cents each.

Barney later remembered those years with fondness: a swarming, raucous yet intimate neighborhood, populated with shopkeepers like Krakow the fishmonger, whose son would grow up to be heavyweight contender Kingfish Levinsky; Finkelstein the butcher, whose son would grow up to be welterweight champion Jackie Fields. Thursday mornings Barney would watch his mother peel six pounds of potatoes for the cholont, a Shabbos delicacy that would cook Friday afternoon in the bakery downstairs and be ready when the family came home from synagogue that evening. On Monday nights his father, who suffered from constant rheumatic pains in his shoulder, would visit the Turkish baths on 14th Street, often bringing Barney and Morrie along to sit in the sweltering steam room and have their backs beaten with oiled oak leaves to increase the circulation, kibitzing and arguing about Talmudic interpretations with an old Russian named Motl.

Under Reb Itchik's eye, there was a strict observance of the ancient laws: not a light switch could be flicked, not a match struck, nor a scrap of toilet paper torn after sundown on Friday (Itchik would in fact bring home the green squares of tissue with which the apples and oranges had been wrapped for use in the family bathroom).

By all accounts, Beryl Rasofsky was an excellent Hebrew student, mastered Rambam and Gemorrah taught by a *cheder*-master named Stein—dubbed "Hinky Dink" by the children, owing to his hobbling on an orthopedic platform shoe. Sarah Rasofsky often marveled that "he could teach the *haftorah* to a stone." After her husband's death, Hinky Dink would become a kind of surrogate father, the man sitting at the head of the Rasofsky family table during Passover Seders and other holiday meals.

2

From similar hardscrabble roots had sprung such luminaries as the bandleader Benny Goodman and Admiral Hyman Rickover, both sons of Maxwell Street tailors; Supreme Court Justice Arthur Goldberg, son of a fruit-and-vegetable peddler; actor Paul Muni, son of the owner of a Yiddish theater; Barney Balaban, the Paramount Pictures mogul; and William Paley, founding president and chairman of the board of CBS. Yet the neighborhood was so notorious for its criminal activity that it became known to the police and crime reporters as "Bloody Maxwell" or "the Bloody Twentieth" (for the old 20th Ward). A 1906 *Chicago Tribune* description of the area claimed that "murderers, robbers, and thieves of the worst kind are born, reared, and grow to maturity in numbers that far exceed the record of any similar district on the face of the globe."

The Jewish mobsters rising from what historian Albert Fried, in *The Rise and Fall of the Jewish Gangster in America*, calls "The Gehenna of the Westside," were "man for man as ferocious as any in the country." Jacob "Greasy Thumb" Guzik, the financial genius of Al Capone's organization, is the most widely known Jewish racketeer to have come from Maxwell Street, but Samuel "Nails" Morton, who owned a garage near the Rasofsky grocery, made a more lasting impression on young Beryl. "Nails was known to be involved in the rackets, so Pa had always forbidden me to have anything to do with him," Ross recalled. "Pa wouldn't even sell him anything when he came into the store." In some respects, Nails Morton—a gangster whose biography reads like something conjured by Isaac Babel—informed Barney Ross's worldview as much as any lesson learned from his Orthodox father.

Morton (1894–1923) was a tall, muscular man who had earned the nickname "Nails," according to crime expert Jay Robert Nash, because of his "tough-as-nails attitude and fighting prowess. Morton also took it upon himself to defend the streets of the Jewish community against invading gangs of other nationalities. Since the area was neglected by the police, Morton would patrol the streets at night with friends, carrying a baseball bat, and woe to anyone who thought to break into the shop of a fellow Jew."

In 1917 he was arrested for nearly beating several members of a rival Polish gang to death and, found guilty of assault with a deadly weapon, given the choice of prison or the military. He enlisted in the 131st Illinois Infantry, which shipped to France as part of the Rainbow Division. In battle he was promoted to sergeant and, according to Nash, "in one engagement, where his company was pinned down by murderous machine-gun fire, Morton led a squad of men through no-man's-land, wiping out an enemy machine-gun nest and clearing a trench full of Germans, capturing twenty men." Wounded twice in the close-quarters fighting, Morton was the only survivor of his squad and was awarded the Croix de Guerre by the French government and promoted to first lieutenant. In his files it was noted that "in addition to possession of natural leadership qualities, Lieutenant Morton has an unusual aptitude for weapons."

Back in Chicago, Morton returned to the rackets, allying himself with the North Side boss Dion O'Bannion, who more than other Chicago mob bosses seems to have had a particularly broad-minded policy of ethnic diversity in his hiring. By 1923, "Nails was one of the most visible and wealthiest bootlegging gangsters in Chicago; earning an estimated $250,000 a year," driving large touring cars and wearing tailor-made suits with special pockets where he could secret his two revolvers. (Morton and Hershie Miller were charged with shooting and killing two Chicago police officers—one had reportedly called Nails a "Jew bastard"—but both racketeers were acquitted of murder on the grounds of self-defense.) He carried an ivory-handled walking stick that concealed a razor-sharp sword, and cut a rakish figure, appeared frequently at prizefights, and was said to own interests in boxers. On May 13, 1923, while riding a horse on the Lincoln Park Bridle Path, Nails was thrown, and kicked in the head by a too-spirited mount. The iron horseshoe caused a skull fracture and Morton died without ever regaining consciousness. Louie "Two Guns" Alterie, one of the O'Bannion mob's top killers, returned to the stable a few days later, asked to rent the same horse, and promptly shot it in the head. (The scene was reenacted in the 1932 film *The Public Enemy*, in which Jimmy Cagney dispatches a horse that has killed his good friend "Nails" Nathan.)

Nails Morton lies today beneath a stone obelisk in Jewish Waldheim Cemetery in Forest Park, a near western Chicago suburb. His death was widely mourned in the Jewish community; as the *Chicago Daily News* reported at the time, "Five thousand Jews paid tribute to Morton as the man who had made the West Side safe for his race. As a young man he had organized a defense society to drive 'Jew baiters' from the West Side."

Despite his father's vehement disapproval, Beryl Rasofsky, chronically undernourished, so short and skinny that his nickname was "Runt," had heard the siren's call of Nails Morton's world. He began a secret life of gambling and petty crime, shooting craps on the corner, stealing gloves and apples and bunches of bananas from pushcarts, engaging in the hand-to-hand wars being fought among the kids on every block.

"Piss on you dirty sheenies," Ross later recalled the rival gangs of Irish, Polish, and Italians taunting. The Jewish boys of Maxwell Street couldn't enter the nearest swimming pool without fighting their way inside. Just to the north, on West Taylor Street, the infamous Italian-American gang known as "the 42's" were wreaking constant terror; the youth gang was to become a kind of farm club for the Mob, with juvenile hoodlums like Sam Giancana eventually rising to the pinnacle of organized crime in Chicago. Whenever Beryl came

Beryl Rasofsky at age fourteen.

back home bearing evidence of this interethnic street fighting, even if he'd only received lumps defending himself, Reb Itchik would be waiting to inflict more damage with a leather cat-o'-nine-tails.

"I got more beatings at home than I got on the streets," Ross told sportswriter Dan Daniel years later. "My parents had the typical Jewish attitude toward fights, black eyes, bloody noses and skull fractures. Mom didn't like to see me come in late for meat and potatoes with bleeding scratches. So I got it but *good*. And I kept right on battling those Italian kids, and a lot of Jewish ones, too."

He found that, in spite of his lack of size or strength, he was an adept street fighter. "I was so fast on my feet and so agile that I was able to get in a few quick punches, then dance and weave so much that my opponent would knock himself out trying to hang one on me," he recalled.

3

On December 13, 1923, ten days short of his fourteenth birthday, Barney was dressing in his ROTC uniform for a morning drill at the Joseph Medill School when a gunshot echoed on Jefferson Street. Rushing downstairs, he heard a cry of "*Gonovim!*" A small crowd had formed around the grocery, and Beryl pushed his way inside. His father lay on the floor, blood soaking through his white apron, shot in the chest. Beryl tore at his father's clothes, ripped off the apron and his shirt and *tzitzis*. "It's alright, Beryl," Itchik said. Ambulance attendants rushed inside the grocery; Beryl heard the sound of his mother shrieking as his father was carried away.

The shooting made the afternoon edition of the *Chicago Daily News:*

GROCER, 60, SHOT IN FIGHT WITH ROBBERS

Two negroes entered the grocery of Isaac Rosofsky, 60 years old, 1303 [inaccurate address but verbatim from news story] Jefferson Street, this morning and purchased 5 cents' worth of apples. The grocer handed the apples to the men and they drew pistols and ordered Rosofsky to "stick them up." The grocer refused to obey and made for the men. He fell in his tracks with a bullet in his chest. Rosofsky's family . . . heard the shot and came out just in time to see the robbers flee south in Jefferson street.

In the county hospital, Itchik hovered in and out of consciousness for thirty-two hours, then, as Barney later remembered, he "awaked once to put a hand on a rheumatic shoulder which had bothered him for years and whisper, 'It doesn't hurt anymore.' " He rubbed his beard and muttered "*Sh'ma Yisroel* [Hear, O Israel]" before dying. The funeral was held in the cramped Rasofsky apartment, women wailing, mirrors draped with blankets. Barney and his older brothers stood to say kaddish and the littlest ones—Sammy, Georgie, and Ida—strained to see their father's casket as it was carried through the crowd on Jefferson Street into the hearse for interment in Jewish Waldheim Cemetery.

In the days following the murder, Sarah Rasofsky fell to pieces. She was hospitalized with a nervous breakdown, said she could no longer bear to live in the apartment across the street from the murder scene. In Barney's memory of the funeral scene, his mother had been so grief-stricken that she tried to throw herself into her husband's open grave. Double-chinned, she is often seen smiling broadly in the photographs from Barney's glory years as a world's champion; yet the pain and rage was forever smoldering. Years later, visiting her husband's grave site—still so observant that she would not go with any of her *kohain* sons, only entering the gates of Jewish Waldheim in the company of nieces and female cousins—she would scare the little girls by convulsing as if in some kind of seizure, shrieking out in inchoate Yiddish rage at her husband's headstone: "Itchik, why did you do this to me?"

Barney's oldest brother Ben, married and working as a bookkeeper, arranged to sell the store and used the money to send his mother to live in Colchester, Connecticut, where Itchik's sister and elderly mother lived. Ben didn't have enough room to take in his other brothers—and his young wife was already pregnant. It was yet another cruel twist in the fate of the Rasofsky clan: Isidore's first grandson, named Yitzhak (Erwin) in his memory, was born a little more than a week after the murder.

Barney and Morrie were sent to live with their father's

cousin Henry Rasof, and the three youngest children were taken in by the Marks Nathan Jewish Orphan Home at Albany and 16th Street. Barney later remembered standing in front of the "gray, dingy-looking orphanage," with fists clenched hard, vowing he would make enough money "to get them out of there."

In his autobiography, *No Man Stands Alone*, published in 1957 (as dictated to coauthor journalist Martin Abramson), Ross says that the two men who killed his father got away with the crime—an elderly customer had witnessed the shooting but was too scared to testify. The killers' escape, in Barney's retelling, fueled his rage at the world, and in every street fight to follow, he could see the faces of the men who murdered his father. "The bitterness and hatred inside me made me a much tougher fighter," he recalled. "Every opponent in a street fight seemed to remind me of Pa's murderers and so I seemed to find extra strength in fighting them, or kicking them in the groin and making them scream in agony."

4

With his mother drifting into madness on the farm in Connecticut, fourteen-year-old Barney lost his pain in the torrent of the Chicago streets. He wandered Roosevelt Road in the clawing cold—"a lost soul," he later said. Technically billeted to his cousin Henry's care, he was a ward of the wild West Side. He started to smoke and curse, and learned he could throw back bootlegged beer like a grown man. He had no time for his oldest brother Ben's lectures, scoffed when Rabbi Stein asked why he hadn't been to *shul*. He screamed that he no longer believed in God.

"In my terrible bitterness and hurt, I wanted to take my feelings out on something, and religion seemed the most logical thing to hit at. Religion had been the biggest thing in Pa's life and what had it gotten him? . . . To teach Hebrew—to have anything to do with religious work—was now the last thing in the world I wanted to do." He stopped wearing *tzitzis* under his shirt, rode the streetcar and handled money on the Sabbath, and began to eat ham and pig's knuckles in restaurants.

"The only Jewish custom I continued to follow was to say the kaddish three times a day. But as far as I was concerned I wasn't doing this for the sake of religion, but merely to pay my respect to Pa and to prevent his remains from turning to dust, which according to ancient belief was what would happen if he wasn't mourned."

He went truant from school, eventually dropped out, and while his friends were at Marshall High, Beryl went to work at a variety of low-paying jobs—a movie-house usher, a stock boy at Sears, Roebuck, as a Maxwell Street "puller," finagling customers into a dry goods store. He developed what would become a lifelong devotion to nightlife—the gruff banter of the pool hall and the clatter of glowing dice on concrete. He ran with a neighborhood gang and worked as muscle in local craps games—if a scrawny boy of pounds can be described as muscle—taking a small percentage on every bet. He became a denizen of the whorehouses of the Haymarket district, and began venturing down to the brothels on the South Side and to the Four Deuces Café (2222 South Wabash), a saloon, gambling den, and brothel run by a Calabrian immigrant named Giacomo (Big Jim) Colosimo, and where a young, hulking transplanted Brooklyn tough named Alphonse Capone had graduated from bartender to bouncer to manager.

Chicago, as Norman Mailer later wrote, "was a town where nobody could forget how the money was made. It was picked up from floors still slippery with blood." We'll probably never know the true extent to which Beryl Rasofsky was "connected" in the illicit rackets of Chicago's West Side. In later years Barney Ross's relationship with "Scarface" Al Capone would be woven into the fabric of his legend, but like so many tales of American gangland, the full truth remains inscrutable.

In *No Man Stands Alone*, Ross says that he worked briefly for the Capone mob during the Prohibition years as a teenage message boy. "Al's knowledge of the things that went on in Chicago was uncanny. He remembered who I was and he knew all the details of Pa's murder. 'The goddamn punks who killed him ought to be thrown in a river full of sharks,' Al said. . . . I was later to find out that though Al Capone was the most ruthless man in the world when it came to fighting people who got in his way, he could be very kind and generous to people he liked." Ross claims that, after a brief spell doing trivial jobs for the boss—fetching cigars, taking shoes to the bootblack, hand-delivering messages to other gangsters—Capone eventually shooed him out of the criminal life with a $20 bill and a warning to "buy your family something and go back to school or get a job. . . . Now beat it before I get mad."

Perhaps these are just the fanciful recollections of an ex-prizefighter trying to weave a colorful yarn (for his co-author Marty Abramson) in his memoirs. We do know that Capone was an avid fan of Barney Ross's, that he and his mob associates frequented Kid Howard's gym as well as the Edmille Health Club, which was in fact owned by Capone's friend Davey "Yiddles" Miller, a former fighter turned referee who had once been shot point-blank in the stomach by the North Side bootlegging boss Dion O'Bannion. And we also know that other popular Maxwell Street–reared fighters like Jackie Fields and King Levinsky would often recall their friendly dialogues with Capone.

Ross himself later disavowed any claim to having been a budding Capone gangster, although throughout his life he openly associated with men closely tied to the Chicago rackets. When Jacob "Sparky" Rubenstein, a close friend of Ross's from the West Side, who, having changed his named to Jack Ruby, was charged with the murder of Lee Harvey Oswald in 1963, the FBI arranged to interview Barney Ross. Several FBI Special Agents pointedly asked if Ross and Ruby had done criminal work for the Capone organization; their report, numbered Exhibit No. 1288 in the Warren Commission volumes on the Kennedy assassination, is almost comic in its trickster's tangle of contradictions:

Ross pointed out that in his autobiography although he stated that he at one time worked for Al Capone, he never did actually work for Capone. . . . He recalled that occasionally Capone would give Ross or one of the members of the group with whom he associated a dollar to run innocuous errands. He mentioned that on several occasions, Capone would give one of them a dollar to deliver an envelope to someone in the downtown section of Chicago. Ross believed that these envelopes, which were sealed, did not contain any messages or anything of value. He believed that Capone did this in order to make them think they were earning a dollar and in order to keep them from hanging around the streets. . . .

More interesting than Barney's possible employment by Capone is that lifelong friendship with Jack Ruby. Ruby was, in an odd way, the Jungian shadow of Ross. In the latter we see the controlled, scientific harnessing of violence; in the former its most undisciplined, impulsive manifestation. Those who knew Barney Ross best could scarcely remember a time when he lost his temper or struck someone in anger; and even in the prize ring he was sometimes chided by sportswriters for lacking the sharklike nature required to finish off a wounded opponent, for not throwing punches with what Mike Tyson, decades later, would memorably call "bad intentions." Ruby, a brawny, balding blowhard who claimed he could "hit harder than Joe Louis," lived most of his life in a cloud of bad intentions, both as a young street tough in Chicago and later as a Dallas nightclub owner known for his incandescent, homicidal fury. Barney's brother George, who'd been friendly with both Jack Ruby and his younger brother Earl (or "Junior"), once told me about a trip to a Chicago Bears game when another fan made the unfortunate mistake of blocking Jack Ruby's car in the Soldier Field lot. Mortified, Georgie watched as Ruby flew into an uncontrollable fury that ended in a physical assault.

Throughout his life, Jack Ruby idolized Barney Ross—carried his water bottle at the gym and lived for the days when he could get into the ring with him to spar. And Ross, for his part, never abandoned his childhood friend, even when Ruby was on trial for first-degree murder.

5

"Boxing," David Remnick observes in his fine Muhammad Ali biography, *King of the World*, "has never been a sport of the middle class. It is a game for the poor, the lottery player, the all-or-nothing-at-all young men who risk their health for the infinitesimally small chances of riches and glory."

Beryl Rasofsky—the prototypical "all-or-nothing-at-all young man"—was fifteen when he first set foot in a professional fight club. Kid Howard—born Howard Cross—was a former prizefighter who ran a small, sweltering gym located on the second floor over a barbershop on the Near South Side. During lunch breaks at his job as a Sears, Roebuck stock boy, Barney came down to watch the men and boys sparring and was intoxicated by the clouds of cigar smoke hovering over the men in fedoras; the fists mummified in billiard cloth and tape; the mineral jelly smeared on gashed eyebrows; the tattoo of leather on leather; the scent of wintergreen and sweat and rubbing alcohol coming from fighters lying flat on their backs for postsparring rubdowns.

He'd come to get a glimpse of another "graduate of the ghetto," Jacob Finkelstein, three years his senior, who had already made a name for himself fighting in Kid Howard's stable. Finkelstein boxed as Jackie Fields; feeling his own surname was too Jewish-sounding, on the spur of the moment he had stolen inspiration from the Marshall Field's department store sign. A quick and skilled tactician, if not a heavy puncher, he would capture the featherweight gold medal at the 1924 Olympic Games in Paris and, later, reign briefly as welterweight champion of the world. Before being eclipsed by Barney Ross, Jackie Fields was the brightest boxing light to emerge from the Maxwell Street ghetto.

For the young street fighters on the Near West Side, a trip to Kid Howard's, nearest of Chicago's numerous fight clubs to the ghetto, became a rite of passage. Inside, one would find a cross section of past and future killers, the loose cannons like Sparky Rubenstein, but also Abraham Lincoln Marovitz, later elected a judge of the United States District Court for the Northern District of Illinois, who boxed for a stint out of Kid Howard's gym, earning small purses in amateur smokers while clerking at a downtown law firm.

On one of his lunchtime visits, Barney mustered his

courage and approached Kid Howard—a tall beefy man known for his natty suits, crisp fedora, and flashing cuff links—and asked for a chance to spar. Howard laughed openly at the underweight West Sider. "You're too scrawny a kid to be a fighter."

Barney persisted, and eventually a tough professional middleweight named Dave Shade stuck a cigar in his mouth and dared the boy to try to knock it out. The prize would be a spot fighting in the windup of an amateur bout. Barney swung wildly as he would in a street fight, throwing looping lefts and rights, but Dave Shade, using elementary boxing science, sidestepped every telegraphed blow. The gym erupted in laughter as Barney whiffed and Dave Shade kept shape-shifting. The next day when Barney returned on his lunch break, he asked for another chance, and now he had cracked pugilism's time-space continuum—throw your punch where your opponent *will be*, not where he is. He managed to smash the cigar into Shade's lip. Kid Howard rewarded Ross with a spot boxing in a three-round windup fight.

He was no natural: His hands were small, wrists narrow, stamina weakened from years of asthma and poor nutrition. As a boy, he had been more than 20 pounds underweight. "I took up the game and trained faithfully," he later wrote in *Fundamentals of Boxing*, his 1943 instructional. "It wasn't long before I could feel my chest expanding, my hands hardening, my body toughening and my mind growing sharper."

He recognized that the mental tools were as crucial as the miles of roadwork and the hours of shadowboxing. "The greatest offensive weapon is a keen mind, the ability to take command of the battle. . . . Only a small part of a champion's greatness lies in his ability. Far more important is his eagerness to learn, his flair for adding finesse and polish to his style."

He later referred to these apprentice years as his era of "pawnshop" fighting, because amateur boxers didn't earn purses, only watches, medals, or pairs of shoes they could sell or pawn for a few dollars. Barney's amateur three-round fights were "wild and unscientific," but he won more fights than he lost, and he soon built a reputation as an exciting scrapper who would give no quarter in the ring. There were so many small fight clubs around Chicago that Barney, in mercenary fashion, began to divide his time between gymnasiums, boxing as many as three or four bouts a week. He would fight midweek at Johnny Cowlan's or Izzy Kline's clubs; in Kid Howard's gym on Saturday nights; Friday nights he'd fight in the Edmille Health Club on Roosevelt Road and Kedzie Avenue, a gym owned by the Capone-connected referee Davey "Yiddles" Miller. Ross was then fighting as a bantamweight—118 pounds. He was still under the legal age of sixteen required by the State Athletic Commission, so he lied about his date of birth.

As a novice fighter, what he lacked in technique he made up for with quick hands and the rock-solid chin that would later, in his long reign as a professional champion, be among his most lauded attributes. He could take almost any opponent's Sunday punch without staggering; indeed, his fighting intensity seemed only to grow when he was hurt. In a good week he might take in $10 or $15, trading his prizes for cash the same day of the bout. His fame was spreading throughout the city. Decades later, reviewing Ross's autobiography in *The New York Times Book Review*, Nelson Algren offered a personal recollection of the young boxer:

> Out of Chicago's ghetto, in the lost summer of 1927, came word that a guy nobody could whip was coming into our own territory to fight. His name was Barney Rasofsky; he weighed 118, and he was going to go to a joint on North Kedzie called Huntinghouse Dancing Academy. He won so easily that I went out and had a pair of boxing gloves tattooed on my arm.

Barney let his brothers Ben and Morrie know the truth about his fighting, and the young boys in the orphanage, George and Sammy, sometimes got permission to leave to sit in the front row during a few of Barney's amateur bouts. But like so many other Jewish fighters, Barney's boxing career remained a secret he zealously guarded from his mother.

By this time, Sarah Rasofsky had recovered sufficiently to return to Chicago where, with Barney and Morrie, she had moved into a small apartment on Roosevelt Road. One night, after a particularly rough amateur bout, when Barney returned home with a cut and swollen lip, she demanded to know who he'd been fighting, but he insisted he'd merely fallen and cut his lip on a curb.

6

Like so many Jewish prizefighters before him, Beryl Rasofsky used a nom de guerre to hide the truth from his overprotective mother. He didn't go to the extreme of Moische Shneir, the welterweight who'd boxed as Mushy Callahan, or Arthur Lieberman, the featherweight who'd fought as Artie O'Leary. Like Jackie Fields and Benny Leonard—né Benjamin Leiner—he chose a neutral-sounding, generically Anglo-American moniker. His older brother, Morrie, had boxed briefly as an amateur—just a handful of times—using the last name Ross, so Barney accepted the hand-me-down mantle.

With only tiny squibs in the daily papers, it was still possible to keep his mother in the dark. But as Barney Ross added to his string of amateur wins, as his following swelled on West Roosevelt Road, it was only a matter of time before Sarah heard the neighborhood gossip about the exploits of Beryl the Terrible. His amateur fights didn't appear in the Chicago edition of the *Forward*, the only paper Sarah read, but his victories began earning two- or three-line mentions in the *Daily News* and the *Tribune*. She confronted him, accused him of lying to her about fighting, and worse, betraying his father's memory. Sixty-five years later, George Rasof—Barney's brothers all legally shortened their surname—vividly recalled for me his mother's attitude about the violent sport. "What was a fighter? To her a fighter was nothing, a *trumbenik*, a *Yiddisheh* bum." This attitude was already a well-established cultural trope; the 1925 silent film *His People* depicts a mother's revulsion with her son's prizefighting:

> A Box-fyteh!? So that's what you become? For this we came to America? So that you should become a Box-fyteh? Better you should be a gangster or even a murderer. The shame of it. A Box-fyteh!

The Hungarian-born historian and sociologist George Eisen, who boxed as a young man in Budapest, has written of the "imperative to acknowledge that in the hierarchy of Jewish religious values, feats of physical prowess were invariably relegated to the 'secular' and the 'mundane.' There has always been a strong aversion in Jewish culture and tradition toward violent or blood sports that often were the hallmarks of neighboring tribes, societies and cultures." The antipathetic attitude toward sport goes back at least as far as the conquest of Judea by Alexander the Great in the fourth century B.C.E., when Jews were first exposed to the sports of boxing and wrestling. One of the more overt signs of Hellenization was the establishment in 174 B.C.E. of a gymnasium in Jerusalem where athletes engaged in sporting activities in the nude. According to the First Book of Maccabees (1:15), some Jewish participants even underwent medical procedures to conceal the fact that they were circumcised. The fact that all Greek games were dedicated to cults deemed idolatrous to Jews—gifts and sacrifices were made to the god Heracles in particular—exacerbated the sense that, for the observant Jew, sport was inextricably linked to the threat of a foreign, pagan culture.

By Barney Ross's youth, the revulsion to violent sport could even be found in the Passover Haggadah's parable of the four boys, the *Arba'ah Banim*, in which we are told of a wise son, a wicked son, a simple son, and a son who cannot even formulate a question. There is an illustration from a 1920 children's Haggadah in which the wicked son—or *rasha*—is depicted as a shirtless, heavily muscled bare-knuckle boxer.

Barney tried to assure his mother that he was no *rasha*, that what he was practicing in that roped-off ring had its own kind of cruel beauty. He was not aiming to make a career of fighting, certainly wasn't yet dreaming of turning professional. But he could earn a lot more pawning a gold watch than he could as a Sears stock boy or working muscle in a Roosevelt Road crap game. In time, she came to accept his choice. Especially when Barney promised her he would only box until he'd made enough money to get Ida, Sam, and

George out of the orphanage, until he could reunite all the Rasofskys under one roof.

7

In 1926, the year Barney Ross began his amateur boxing career, another brash young midwesterner who liked to wrap his fists in billiard cloth published a dazzling first novel about American expatriates in Paris and Pamplona. *The Sun Also Rises*, the book that first made Ernest Hemingway into a literary star, begins with a description of a Jewish boxer, modeled on Hemingway's erstwhile friend, tennis partner, and romantic rival Harold Loeb:

> Robert Cohn was once middleweight boxing champion of Princeton. He cared nothing for boxing, in fact he disliked it, but he learned it painfully and thoroughly to counteract the feeling of inferiority he'd felt on being treated as a Jew at Princeton. There was a certain inner comfort in knowing he could knock down anybody who was snooty to him, although being very shy, and a thoroughly nice boy, he never fought, except in the gym.

The first time I read *The Sun Also Rises*, an undergraduate at Princeton myself, I was more than a little mortified and wanted to drop the white paperback into the fountain in front of the Woodrow Wilson School. It wasn't just the liberal peppering of the word "kike," an epithet which Hemingway seems to love putting in his characters' mouths, and which also appears with alarming regularity in his personal letters to friends. I think what unsettled me most about the Robert Cohn character was the way in which he seems both a distillation and a willful distortion of the long tradition of the "scientific" Jewish boxer. As Hemingway renders him, Cohn is a skilled fighter, yet a wholly unmanly one. He doesn't obey the laws of Hemingway's masculine ethos, doesn't drink hard, hates hunting and fishing, nearly vomits on himself when he witnesses the gory bullfighting in Pamplona. His most telling gesture is to remove his eyeglasses, almost daintily, before challenging Jake Barnes, the novel's narrator and Hemingway's obvious alter ego, to a fistfight.*

One would scarcely realize it, reading Hemingway today, but by 1928, writes Allen Bodner in his oral history *When Boxing Was a Jewish Sport*, "Jews were the dominant nationality in professional prizefighting, followed by the Italians and Irish." Through the twenties and thirties, an estimated one-third of all professional boxers in the United States were

---

*Hemingway, a newsman before he was a novelist, did know the facts. He had followed boxing avidly from his boyhood in Oak Park and, as a young reporter for the *Toronto Star*, had been present at the New York Hippodrome in 1922 when Benny Leonard, then reigning lightweight champ, had fought welterweight king Jack Britton. He was so incensed at the way the fight had ended—Leonard, who'd been winning the fight going into the thirteenth round, fouled Britton with a low blow, then struck him before he could rise, causing widespread rumors that the fight had been fixed by Jewish gamblers—that, according to Hemingway biographers, he was moved to pen "Fifty Grand," a short story depicting a professional fight fixed by Jewish prizefighting promoters and gangsters.

Jewish. Novelist and screenwriter Budd Schulberg recalls how boys of his generation "felt a special surge of pride when the wearers of the six-pointed star on their trunks proved their mettle" in the ring against other ethnic fighters. Indeed, Arthur Brisbane, the famed newspaperman, once said of Benny Leonard, "He has done more to conquer anti-Semitism than a thousand textbooks."

And there is a stark dichotomy in this heyday of Jewish prizefighting. The sport was at once hugely popular among the working-class immigrants (boxing lessons were offered at the Educational Alliance on the Lower East Side), and 60,000 were in attendance at Yankee Stadium when Benny Leonard fought Lew Tendler, the powerful southpaw from Philadelphia, for the world's lightweight championship in 1922. Yet the exploits of Jewish champions like Leonard were rarely reported in the Yiddish press or much noted among the intellectual class. Irving Howe's *World of Our Fathers*, with its seemingly comprehensive chronicling of immigrant life on the Lower East Side, contains only one passing thirteen-word reference to Jewish prizefighting: "Benny Leonard was proving that a Jew could be the champion lightweight boxer."

Leonard himself had written in 1925, "I believe that the Jew is especially adapted for the sport of boxing because, in the final analysis, it is the most elemental form of self-defense." It was a thesis that had first been promulgated by Daniel

HUMPHRIES & MENDOZA,

their third public contest for Superiority, on Sept. 29: 1790.

Daniel Mendoza (*left*), "The Light of Israel,"
the first of the great Jewish pugilists.

Mendoza (1763–1836), the Sephardic Jew billed as "The Light of Israel" (and sometimes simply as "Mendoza the Jew") who reigned as the Sixteenth Champion of the London Prize Ring.

Mendoza fought in the bare-knuckle era, when the sport of boxing was more akin to human cockfighting than our modern version: eye-gouging, hair-pulling, and below-the-belt blows were all then legal. It was also a time of no weight divisions, and despite his small stature (five feet seven and 160 pounds, the size of a small middleweight today), Mendoza regularly defeated men 50 pounds heavier. He had grown up poor in the Whitechapel district, worked as a glass cutter, laborer, assistant to a greengrocer, and an actor before making a career of fighting. "I was here frequently drawn into contests with butchers and others in the neighbourhood, who, on account of my mistress being of the Jewish religion, were frequently disposed to insult her," he wrote in his memoirs.

According to Pierce Egan, the seminal chronicler of British boxing of the early nineteenth century (worshiped by *New Yorker* writer A. J. Liebling and the man credited with coining the phrase "sweet science of bruising"), Mendoza was a "complete artist" and a "star of the first brilliancy." If not the originator—Mendoza himself, as skilled at the art of self-promotion as he was at the art of self-defense, often made the claim—he was certainly among the first boxers to incorporate what we now consider the staples of the sport: jabbing, sidestepping footwork, and defensive sparring. Mendoza's speed, technique, and agility allowed him to triumph over stronger and far larger opponents. (One interesting, if wholly unprovable theory, is that he may have incorporated aspects of fencing techniques, at which the Jews of medieval Spain were said to be particularly accomplished.)

He published a book, *The Art of Boxing*, and developed a loyal following that spread far beyond the Jews of the East End. The Prince of Wales and the Duke of York are reported to have attended his fights, and Mendoza was by some accounts the first Jew in English history to speak to a king when he was granted an audience with George III at Windsor. Fighters of the era generally wore their hair close-cropped, but Mendoza, perhaps styling himself a Samson-like figure, was famous for dark flowing locks. In his final fight in 1795, he was knocked out by the 200-pound John Jackson, who won the fight by gripping Mendoza by the hair and bashing his face bloody.

In Mendoza's wake came a string of accomplished Jewish boxers—"of late, the Jews are becoming the bullies of the people of London," reads one magazine account from 1810—such as Sam Elias, known as "Dutch Sam" and "the Terrible Jew," a spry 130-pounder who claimed to train on three glasses of gin, three times a day. He also claimed to have invented the uppercut. Other English Jews who fought in the ring in this era were Barney Aaron ("the Star of the East"); Henry Abrahams; the four Belasco brothers—Abraham, Israel, Samuel, and John; Isaac Bittoon; Elisha Crabbe; Abraham da Costa; Barnard Levy; Keely Lyons; Daniel Martin; Isaac Mousha; Abraham Robes; Solomon Sodicky; and two cousins of Daniel Mendoza's, Angel Hyams and Aaron

Mendoza. Their exploits were carried along the streets of the East End in popular ballads:

> Cutler Street is like a fair;
> Barney Aaron! Barney Aaron!
> All the little Jews declare,
> Rows his keel like Charon
> Old Mendoza—Young Mendoza
> Both are known and famed in fight . . .

By the end of the nineteenth century, the United States had supplanted the British Isles as the leading center for boxing. Fighters from impoverished Irish neighborhoods, such as heavyweight champion John L. Sullivan, were dominant for a generation. Then, with the mass migration of some 2 million East European Jews to the United States in the late nineteenth and early twentieth centuries, the teeming ghettos of the Lower East Side and Maxwell Street spawned a second golden era of Jewish prizefighting, producing the likes of the San Francisco heavyweight contender "Chrysanthemum" Joe Choynski (though only 170 pounds, judged by Jack Johnson to have thrown some of the hardest punches in the division, and often called "finest heavyweight to never win a championship"), and the Lower East Side's Leach Cross (Louis Wallach, known as "the Fighting Dentist" because he had graduated from New York University's School of Dentistry). Bantamweight Harry "the Human Hairpin" Harris was the first Jewish boxer to win a world championship under Marquis of Queensberry rules, reigning briefly in 1901–2. There were hundreds of other

In Stillman's Gymnasium on Eighth Avenue, four Jewish boxing greats give Ross the benefit of their years of experience as he prepares for the lightweight championship rematch with Tony Canzoneri, August 1933. From left to right: Sid Terris, Ross, Al Singer, Benny Leonard, and Leach Cross.

prominent Jewish champions and contenders in the early decades of the last century, including light heavyweights Battling Levinsky, Slapsie Maxie Rosenbloom, Bob Olin, Yale Okun, and Abie Bain; middleweights Al McCoy, Ben Jeby, Georgie Abrams, Solly Krieger, Dave Rosenberg, and Phil Kaplan; welterweights Ted "Kid" Lewis, Harry Lewis, Jackie Fields, Mushy Callahan; lightweights Lew Tendler, Charley White, Jackie "Kid" Berg, Sid Terris, Ruby Goldstein, and Al "The Bronx Beauty" Singer; featherweights Abe Attell, Benny Bass, and Joey Sangor; bantamweights Abe Goldstein, Newsboy Brown, Young Montreal, Charley

Goldman, and Charley "Phil" Rosenberg; and flyweights "Corporal" Izzy Schwartz, Victor "Young" Perez, Johnny Rosner, and Jackie "Kid" Wolfe.

Though it's little remarked upon today, the influence of the pioneering fighters of London's East End still permeated the sport into the mid-1930s, and during Barney Ross's reign as welterweight champion of the world, it was not uncommon for American newspapermen to refer to Jewish fighters as "Disciples of Mendoza."

8

In the winter of 1929, as Barney Ross was training to enter the Golden Gloves tournament, the wars of the Windy City's Prohibition gangsters were reaching their grisly crescendo. The Thompson submachine gun, savage weapon of choice among bootleggers, had become so synonymous with the city that it had been dubbed the "Chicago typewriter." On February 14, gunmen in the employ of Al Capone, in their botched attempt to assassinate North Side boss George "Bugs" Moran, slaughtered seven men in the S-M-C Cartage Company garage on North Clark Street. Barney Ross later claimed that the St. Valentine's Day Massacre "meant more to me than it did to most people," since he knew each of the men who were murdered personally. A fanciful embellishment, most likely, but not entirely far-fetched. The gym in which he trained for the Golden Gloves, the Edmille Health Club on Kedzie Avenue, owned as it was by Capone's man Davey Miller, was housed over a restaurant frequented by numerous notorious gangland figures. And Ross, by his own admission, was still dabbling in a life of petty crime, running errands for West Side bookmakers and bootleggers.

Davey Miller sponsored Barney Ross in the Golden Gloves, then a relatively new amateur tournament. First staged in the Chicago Coliseum in 1923, the competition was the brainchild of Arch Ward, the *Tribune* sportswriter, editor, and promoter sometimes called the "Cecil B. DeMille of Sports," owing to the fact that he had a hand in conceiving and staging the first all-star baseball and college football games. Barney Ross entered in the 1929 Golden Gloves at featherweight (126 pounds), fighting in the stable of Miller's Edmille Health Club. Despite his growing record of amateur wins—one early news story refers to "Barney Ross, the up-and-coming West Side Jew Kid" the local sportswriters hadn't yet pegged him as the cream of the tournament; another Jewish pugilist from the West Side ghetto, Harry Garbell, fighting at bantamweight, was touted as that year's best young prospect.

In front of a crowd of 9,000 in the Coliseum, Barney scored a knockout over a fighter named Mike Pallard, beat Art Donovan on points in the semifinals, then emerged the champion in a fast-paced three-rounder with Jackie Davis.

The local heroes were bound for New York, which had its own version of the tournament sponsored by the *Daily News*. The two cities would pit their respective Golden Glovers in a single night of head-to-head matchups to determine the

Intercity Champions. On the eve of the train trip to New York, Barney earned his first substantial write-up in the *Chicago Tribune*—BARNEY ROSS HAS BIG ASSET; IT'S A WICKED LEFT HAND—complete with a doe-eyed photo of the twenty-year-old with a thick black swatch of hair sweeping boyishly over his left eye. "Ross is a self-made boxer," remarked Jack Eile, his trainer at the Edmille Health Club. "When he came to our club he showed little ability. He was willing to learn and never flinched when he was hit. I showed him how to jab and hook with his left and how to clinch."

The Intercity bouts were held in the Mecca of the prize-fighting world, Madison Square Garden—then located on 51st Street and 8th Avenue—on March 27, 1929. It was a capacity crowd of 20,000—and according to a New York *Daily News* estimate, more than 15,000 eager fans had to be turned away at the doors, with a small army of New York policemen mounted on horseback trying to control the overeager mob. When the Chicago team's favorite, Harry Garbell, lost his bantamweight bout, the spotlight turned to Barney Ross, who was paired off against a quick, strong New Yorker named Al Santora. "I didn't feel very good when I started for the ring," Barney recalled. "The two Chicago boys just ahead of me had both lost and come back to the dressing-room in tears." Santora and Ross battled to a draw after three rounds, and the judges ordered a fourth, tie-breaking round. Barney didn't feel he could stand up for another minute, but he summoned some extra reserve and, in the final decision, was awarded the 126-pound Intercity amateur title. Interviewed later by *The Ring*, he said, "That fight taught me something I never will forget—that no matter how bad off you may be, the other fellow may be worse."

The New York team won eleven of the sixteen bouts, but even in a losing cause, Barney's star status had been made in New York. The *Daily News* had singled him out as "the ace of the visitors . . . a keen-eyed chap with a wavy mop of black hair." The Chicago team's every move in New York had been avidly followed by the press: their boat ride up the Hudson; the trip to the peak of the Woolworth Building to gaze at the city (the Golden Glovers "spat daintily upon it," it was reported); their prefight trip to unwind at the Roxy movie palace watching the Marx Brothers' latest comedy, *Animal Crackers.*

Back in Chicago, the sportswriters began to murmur about Barney Ross's chances in the professional ranks. The transition is not as logical as it now appears. "Amateur boxing compares with professional boxing as college theatricals compare with stealing scenes from Margaret Rutherford," A. J. Liebling once wrote in the *New Yorker.* Barney Ross was, as in so many things, the trailblazer: the first Golden Glover to go on to win a professional championship. He was followed several years later by a light heavyweight from Detroit named Joe Louis, and a host of other professional Hall of Famers that included Cassius Clay and Sugar Ray Leonard.

Barney harbored no lofty dreams. "I became a pro for the same reason I became an amateur," he recalled years later, long after his retirement. "I had no hopes or goal of a big time success—my object was simply to keep going until I could put away enough money to bring the kids out of the orphanage and support them till they were old enough to support themselves."

9

Jackie Fields, three years his senior, son of a Maxwell Street butcher, was Barney's stablemate and mentor. The very week that Barney captured the Intercity amateur championship, Fields had won the National Boxing Association's welterweight title against Young Jack Thompson; four months later, he beat Joe Dundee to capture the undisputed world welterweight belt. Fields hired Barney at a rate of $5 a round to work as his sparring partner as he trained for an over-the-weight match in Detroit. "I take pride in saying I was a good teacher to him," Fields told sportswriter Ira Berkow in 1975 when he was then working as a tuxedo-clad "casino host" at the Sands Hotel in Las Vegas. "I told him to stay in shape because half the guys can't go ten rounds at top speed. And if you can, you're the boss. I'd say, 'Get your hands up a little higher,' or 'Jab it out a little stronger.' Instead of tappin'. Jab in. Hook 'em. Jab 'em. But I taught him the first thing, 'Be careful of the stooges around you. They hang with you because you're Barney Ross. They'll suck your blood.' And sorry to say they did."

Barney began his professional fighting career in preliminaries to Fields's fights. When Jackie traveled to the West Coast to fight out of the Main Street Gym in Los Angeles,

Barney followed him, and had his first professional fight against a Mexican fighter named Ray Lugo on September 1, 1929. Barney was outweighed by 6 pounds. It was a far cry from the packed Golden Gloves Intercity finals in Madison Square Garden, where a throaty Manhattan throng had urged the Jewish fighter on. In Los Angeles, on the early undercard, the Main Street Gym was half-empty and the crowd quickly turned ugly. Barney heard catcalls of "Kill the dirty little Jew." Nervous and overcautious, Ross outboxed Lugo and, though barely able to stand by the end of the sixth round, the Jewish fighter took the decision and his first professional purse: $75. A week later he'd notched up his second win, in the same gym, against Joe Borola, this time winning $25 more.

Back in Chicago, the referee and gang leader Davey Miller teamed Barney up with the partnership who would manage him for the rest of his career, a pair of seasoned fight men named Pian and Winch. Sam "Pi" Pian was Jewish but with his thick black hair swept back with Pomade, was often taken for Italian; he was the business end of the operation. Cornerman Art Winch—bald, short, pear-shaped, with baggy pants cinched up high on his rib cage—was an Italian who was often assumed to be a Jew. Pi and Winch were impressed with Barney's amateur record, but they initially refused to manage him as a pro, because they'd also heard about his street reputation—knew that he used to run crap games, was said to be obstinate and hard to control.

For the next three years Barney fought on undercards in Knights of Columbus halls and arenas around the Midwest,

Ross in training camp.

running through a string of featherweight and lightweight competition, knocking out Young Terry and Harry Dublinsky and Lou Perez and Petey Mack.

He wasn't yet a headliner and the purses remained small, especially when, as he later recalled in his memoirs, "Old Man Depression knocked the bottom out of the box office"; but he kept bringing in the $100 paydays and cobbling together enough money to set his mother up in a larger apartment on Roosevelt Road. He still hadn't saved up enough to get Ida, Sam, and George out of the orphanage, but the boys were allowed out with chaperones so that they could see their brother's fights.

Pian and Winch had him training in George Trafton's Gym in the Loop, a fifth-floor prizefighting club located across the street from the Palace Theater and Bismark Hotel (Trafton was a former all-pro guard with the Chicago Bears). The elevator was rickety, and on the younger brothers' first trip up to the fifth-floor gym, Barney warned George and Sam not to get out on the fourth floor by mistake: it was a bookie joint run by the infamous Jewish gangland figure Charles "Babe" Barron.

"Barney Ross, outstanding Chicago lightweight of the present season, appears for the second time in a Cicero Stadium headliner tonight when he meets Jackie Davis," wrote the *Chicago Tribune* on March 20, 1931. On October 21, 1932, in his first main event at the Chicago Stadium, Ross beat Battling Battalino, the former featherweight champion, in a ten-round decision. Then on March 22, 1933, at the Chicago Coliseum, he scored a ten-round decision over the number-one lightweight contender, Billy "The Fargo Express" Petrolle, and Arch Ward, in the *Tribune*, predicted, "It looks like young Barney Ross, whose real name is Rasofsky, can't escape the 135 pound championship." The victory over Billy Petrolle—a future Hall of Famer—set up a matchup with Tony Canzoneri and the first in a series of round-robins that would go down in boxing folklore as the most exciting championship bouts in the sport's history.

PART TWO

1

They have been called boxing's Holy Trinity—Canzoneri, Ross, and McLarnin—the trio of future Hall of Famers who would dominate the lighter weight divisions in the 1930s, when those weight classes were widely regarded as far more competitive than the typically marquee heavyweight class, in the doldrums when it came to champions. They couldn't have been more perfectly scripted by Hollywood; "Tough Tony" Canzoneri, a curly-headed Italian-American from Brooklyn by way of New Orleans; Jimmy "The Baby-faced Assassin" McLarnin, originally from County Down, Ulster, now fighting out of Vancouver, British Columbia; and Barney Ross, the Lower East Side–born, Maxwell Street–reared "Pride of the Ghetto."

In the classic era of tribal fight fans, each boxer's management played the ethnic card to the hilt: Canzoneri would hop through the ropes to the strains of a tarantella; McLarnin, to an Irish jig; Barney Ross, to the tearjerker "My Yiddishe Momme." Ross always avoided the obvious symbol of the Star of David on his trunks—like his idol Benny Leonard. His shorts were emblazoned with a simple "B.R." Yet there was unmistakable symbolism in the inexpensive striped blue-and-white terrycloth robe that he wore throughout his career for good luck.

His own mother by now had made her peace with Berchik's chosen profession; indeed, she'd become one of his most public boosters. If she stayed home to listen to the fights on the radio, she would be nearly frantic with worry, so she made herself a fixture at all his big battles in the Chicago Stadium and the Coliseum. Since Friday night was the big professional fight night, and since she honored her slain husband's memory by remaining observant, she would insist on walking the entire distance home, usually accompanied by several dozen of Barney's friends and supporters from Roosevelt Road.

Tony Canzoneri, in Barney's later estimation, was the most gifted boxer he ever faced in his career. Some experts thought Billy Petrolle and Jimmy McLarnin may have wielded harder right hands, and Henry Armstrong may have been the indefatigable "perpetual motion machine," but no fighter was more thrilling to watch than Canzoneri. The popular Louisiana-born boxer with the broad smile and tightly curled black hair stood five feet five and fought with a feline grace and an intuitive technique that broke all the conventions of the "sweet science."

It's hard today to appreciate how dazzlingly unorthodox Canzoneri must have seemed. As every young boxer learns, one of the cardinal mistakes is to lower your guard and give your opponent a clean shot at the chin; we have grainy newsreels in which Tony Canzoneri seems to be bobbing and dancing for fifteen rounds with both hands held well below his waist. As Ross wrote in *Fundamentals of Boxing*, "Canzoneri had an unorthodox style. He kept his guard down and he waved his face about, offering a teasing target. But he alone knew how to handle himself in that set-up in such a way that there was no danger to him. He alone knew how to take his face away in the nick of time and pummel his foe freely when the chance presented itself. . . . As Benny Leonard often said, 'Do not be an imitation of a man like Canzoneri, at least not a bad imitation. His tricks will probably die with him.' "

He was astonishingly quick—perhaps quicker even than Barney Ross, considered a lightning flash of a boxer himself—and when the two men signed for a lightweight title bout, after Barney's impressive ten-round win against Billy Petrolle, the matchup was touted as a meeting of the two most talented lightweights to meet since Benny Leonard fought Lew Tendler. "Ross is the cleverest and most competent young fellow in the ring today," one sportswriter wrote in 1932. "He is a sharpshooter, a jolting puncher, wastes no motions and can box. Can he take it?"

Canzoneri, listed as only one year older than Barney—there's some dispute about his actual year of birth—had been a professional fighter since his teenage years in Brooklyn and was featherweight champion of the world before Barney even entered the Golden Gloves. In November 1930, Canzoneri knocked out Al Singer in sixty-six seconds, the quickest ending to a lightweight title bout ever. That set up

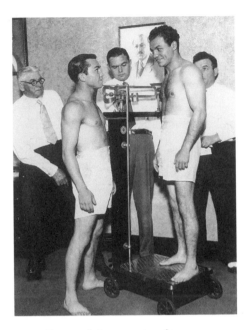

Ross and Canzoneri exchange
none-too-menacing stares during
the official weigh-in.

his showdown with junior-welterweight champion Jackie "Kid" Berg, the tiny whirlwind fighting out of London's Jewish Whitechapel section, a cockney heir to the school of Daniel Mendoza and Dutch Sam. Canzoneri scored a third-round knockout, walked away with two title belts, and in the judgment of Nat Fleischer's *The Ring* magazine was the best pound-for-pound fighter in the world.

Ross and Canzoneri squared off for the first time on Friday, June 23, 1933, in a ten-round title bout at the Chicago Stadium. The flyer billed the fight as "Chicago's Premier

World's Fair Fistic Attraction," with tickets ranging from $2.40 to $7.50. The official attendance was listed as 11,204. Little George and Sammy were let out of the orphanage on a chaperoned furlough so they could attend the fight. Ma Rasofsky had left long before sundown, so that she wouldn't desecrate the Sabbath; in fact, the tiny woman with the failing eyesight had become a character herself in the fight's promotion; one cartoonist had depicted the Ross-Canzoneri championship as a war between the Jewish and Italian mothers. She and her sons sat seven or eight rows back, the ringside seats being filled by politicians, celebrities, and silk-suited gangsters from the Capone organization and Jewish gamblers like Babe Barron and Lovin' Putty Annixter.

The betting odds, which had remained stable at 2 to 1 for the reigning lightweight champion, shorted on the day of the fight, with Canzoneri installed as a 6 to 5 favorite. He was thought to have more knockout power, but Barney had the better ring craft, the more classic boxer's style. It was billed as the biggest fight to be staged in Chicago since the infamous Tunney-Dempsey "Long Count" championship at Soldier Field. Decades later sportswriter Jack Griffin left us a vivid portrait of the Ross form at its peak: "A slim kid . . . with glossy patent-leather hair, he had the movements of a ballet dancer. The left would come out, hooking, jabbing and then that right, cocked against his cheek, would fire, straight on target."

For the first six rounds, Canzoneri seemed to have the fight under control; as Barney entered the seventh, both eyes were cut badly, and the heavy stream of blood made it hard for him to see. "Nevertheless," as *The Ring* magazine's ringside reporter Frank Maestro put it, "the dark-eyed, raven-haired Chicago lad . . . with the fire of youth and ambition in his eyes, suddenly found inspiration and lashed a two-fisted attack that turned the trick for him." It was an exceedingly close decision—the judges, William Battye and Edward Hintz, scored the fight for Ross, while referee Tommy Gilmore saw the ten-rounder as even. The boys from Roosevelt Road and Maxwell Street, shoulder-to-shoulder in the cheap seats, shouted themselves hoarse when the announcement came that Barney Ross was now a dual world's champion, holder of the lightweight and junior-welterweight belts, the first boxer in history to ever capture two titles in one night of fighting. Canzoneri complained bitterly he'd been robbed by biased judges, and many of the New York sportswriters in attendance shared the view.

2

The lion's share of the purse, some $30,000 went to Canzoneri; but Barney Ross's payday of over $11,000 was the most money he had ever seen in one lump sum. More important than winning the championship, he often said later, was the fact that he had finally achieved the goal he had set for himself ever since his father's murder had split up the family. With his winnings he had set his mother up in a sprawling six-room apartment with double plumbing on Independence Boulevard near Roosevelt Road—due west of the Maxwell

Street ghetto. The boulevard, near Douglas Park, had become among the most fashionable addresses for Chicago's striving Jews. Over the span of several months—not as Barney later simplified the story, in one single, celebratory night—he was able to bring his three young siblings out of the orphanage: Ida first, followed by Sam, and Georgie, the last to come out of Marks Nathan in January 1933, and the family was finally reunited under one roof. On hot nights Ma Rasofsky would sleep outside on the open porch. Barney would play the piano; the Yiddish melodies would drift out over Independence Boulevard.

Other nights he would roam, swaggering in his hand-tailored suits, socks always matching his silk pocket square, laughing, as Carl Sandburg wrote of that wide prairie city, "the stormy, husky, brawling laughter of Youth." Now the curious flocked to Trafton's Gym to watch him shadowboxing, the "Hebrew Flash" doing skipping routines so intricate that the jump rope appeared to become a kind of hissing viper. Girls he'd never met sent him offers of marriage. He held court in plush suites at the Morrison Hotel—which became a second home for Ross and his entourage—and at night he partied at the Chez Paree and Big Jim Colosimo's, rubbing shoulders with the "swellest society folk from the Gold Coast" (the prestige address of Lake Shore Drive), as well as the gangland figures he'd known since his boyhood in the ghetto. Al Capone had been jailed on a tax-evasion conviction—en route to his ignominious end as a syphilitic inmate of Alcatraz—but his brothers, Ralph and Matty, were avid fans of Barney Ross, as were other organized crime heavies like Frank Nitti, Murray "the Camel" Humphries, the Fischetti brothers, and Julius "Lovin' Putty" Annixter, the Jewish gambling kingpin, who bestowed on Ross a bejeweled Longines watch as tribute for having defeated Tony Canzoneri.

But another infamous Jewish gangland figure was not in the hometown boy's corner: Charles "Babe" Barron, who ran the sports book on the fourth floor in the same building as Trafton's Gym, had lost a fortune on the decision and physically accosted Joseph Triner, chairman of the Illinois State Boxing Commission. Babe Barron, sometimes known as "the Colonel" because he had been commissioned at that rank in the Army, was the sort of picaresque Chicagoan who deserves more than the two-line mentions in organized-crime histories. A former bantamweight boxing contender himself, he had been charged with murdering a rival racketeer named John Walsh in 1929 ("the shooting followed a fist fight between Barron and Walsh at the Chicago stadium, when the two quarreled over the merits of some of the pugilists," wrote the *Tribune*), though he successfully pleaded self-defense and avoided prison; in the postwar years Barron fronted various mob-controlled casinos in Havana, and was regarded by law-enforcement experts as the Chicago Outfit's handpicked man in the Sands Hotel and Casino in Las Vegas.

Babe Barron was like a brother to Tony Canzoneri, and after the much-heralded Ross-Canzoneri rematch at the Polo Grounds in New York, Barron again vented his rage on the unfortunate Triner, who, we can safely assume, Babe suspected of using undue influence on the judge's scorecards.

As the boxing commissioner was coming out of Canzoneri's dressing room, he was punched in the head by the hot-blooded Babe, who shouted, "Why, you dirty burglar!" before being grabbed by the police and escorted out of the Polo Grounds. Triner declined to file charges and tried to keep the story quiet, but when it broke in bold type in the *Chicago Daily News*—TRINER HIT BY GAMBLER—the commissioner offered a dry riposte: "Tell my friends I am still alive."

The blood feud made for the sort of public-relations bonanza that boxing promoters had been craving since the bare-knuckle days of Daniel Mendoza, the Light of Israel, and Dutch Sam, the Terrible Jew. But Canzoneri, with his Jewish manager, and Ross, with his mixed Jewish-Italian handlers, were already loosening the bonds of conventional ethnic rivalry. This was as much Chicago versus New York as it was Jew versus Italian. Certainly, the tug of ethnic identity could be felt inside the Stadium, but these allegiances lived alongside larger affiliations—in ten years the country itself would be at war, and Barney would become simply an *American* hero.

Pian and Winch agreed to a rematch immediately after the Chicago Stadium fight, but Barney insisted that it take place in New York City, if only to clear up any lingering doubts that he may have benefited from a hometown bias. The handlers also demanded that this time Barney get a guaranteed $30,000 purse. Disgruntled by the negotiations, Sammy Goldman, Canzoneri's manager, went to the press with stories that Barney knew he'd been beaten in the first fight and was afraid to give Canzoneri a rematch until "six solid citizens called upon Ross's managers and persuaded them to go through with their promise of a New York bout." We'll probably never know for certain if there's any truth to this story, whether Babe Barron's boys had used strong-arm tactics to force the rematch; evidence to the contrary is pretty substantial: that throughout his championship reign, Barney Ross was never known to duck competition, and whenever judges' decisions were in doubt, he did not hesitate to sign for a prompt rematch.

That second Ross-Canzoneri bout, September 12, 1933, was a glowing gladiatorial spectacle at Coogan's Hollow. More than 50,000 people came out to the Polo Grounds; the ring on the infield was lit up with twenty-nine 1,000-watt lamps, and members of the New York Giants football team, dressed in full uniform, worked as ushers guiding the notables to their ringside seats: the members of Roosevelt's cabinet, Governor Lehman, and New York mayor O'Brien; Al Jolson camped in the third row, and Babe Ruth sat with Damon Runyon and Grantland Rice in the press section. Most of the fans in the bleachers had traveled on the 8th Avenue subway, and paper arrows taped to lampposts had guided the way to the ballpark. (In a surreal touch, the Polo Grounds was filled with massive backdrops depicting scenes from the Hebrew Bible, left over from the dress rehearsal for *The Romance of a People*, a sprawling pageant depicting all 4,000 years of Jewish history and scheduled for the night after the championship, in part as a response to the recent Nazi pogroms in Germany. September 14 had been officially declared "Jewish Day," by New York mayor O'Brien.)

As the fighters made their entrances, pearl-grey fedoras bobbed expectantly and wisps of cigar smoke swirled into the night sky. Canzoneri was first through the ropes, weighing 133½ pounds, hopping lightly in his black-satin robe. Barney slipped in through the same corner as Tony, at an even 135, dressed in his familiar frayed blue-and-white bathrobe. He was jittery, never having fought before so large an audience, and a boisterous, fight-savvy New York crowd at that. He wondered if he would have the stamina for a scheduled fifteen-rounder, the first time he'd trained for that grueling distance. Tough Tony was the local favorite, but a hearty ovation swept through the Polo Grounds when Barney was introduced as reigning lightweight champ. Izzy Kline and Art Winch were Barney's seconds. Barney later recollected that Kline, noting the extraordinary number of Jews in attendance, broke the tension with a wisecrack about how many of the tribe would be dead if Nazi thugs could have set off a bomb on Coogan's Bluff. A joke—yet not altogether funny, with a classically Jewish nod to the rising tide of anti-Semitism.

From the opening bell, it was a furious melee, neither man wasting any energy on defense: now Barney stunned by a Canzoneri right to the solar plexus; now Cazoneri rocked by clean hooks to the body and chin; both bulling constantly forward, slugging, clinching, trying to be the first to land on the break. By the thirteenth round, Ross was swinging as if in a Maxwell Street brawl. Canzoneri landed low blows in Rounds Six, Eight, and Nine. To the surprise of many, it was the defending champion, as Paul Gallico wrote in the New York *Daily News*, "who outslugged Tony, beat him in the rallies and exchanges, made him stop, and who came blazing back when stung or hurt, so much so that he offset every advantage that Tony could get." The pace had begun to tell on Tony Canzoneri; his body was discolored and covered in welts, and he seemed ready to drop with fatigue. In the fifteenth, Canzoneri unleashed his heaviest shot of the night—a right to Ross's head. But Barney answered with a two-fisted barrage, and with each punch he screamed curses, along with exhortations for Tony to fall. Through swollen lips Canzoneri cursed back at Ross. They were swinging until the final bell, arms thrown around each other. It was a split decision: George Kelly scored the fight for Canzoneri, Harold Barnes for Ross, and referee Arthur Donovan cast the deciding vote for "the winner and *still* lightweight champion of the world. . . ." Canzoneri's elderly father climbed into the ring, grabbed a stool, and was trying to hurl it at one of the judges when he was muscled away by a policeman.

Few experts doubted the validity of the verdict. In the final analysis, the Jewish fighter's crisp left hand proved to be the decisive weapon—he used the straight left like a master fencer, and his methodical sidestepping and pivoting can still be studied as a primer on boxing footwork. Indeed, Nat Fleischer, editor of *The Ring*, judged Barney's left hand to be as good as Benny Leonard's. The skeptical New York sportswriters, some of whom had derided Barney as a "cheese champion," viewed Ross's victory as justly deserved; Gallico, in the New York *Daily News*, went so far as to declare:

> The new champion is the better man. He defended his
> newly won title a few short months after he acquired it.
> He moved into the enemy's own territory and took him
> at a longer distance. He matched him at every turn and
> then beat him, beat him at boxing, but chiefly beat him
> at fighting. The kid's a gambler. He's a fight lover, a boy
> who likes the rough going, and fights best when he has
> been hurt.

The next day Ross and his mother, in their suite in the New Yorker Hotel, were swarmed by well-wishers and reporters. Ross, dressed in a well-cut dark blue suit, his nose swollen from the fifteen-rounder, announced that he was planning to return to the Polo Grounds that night, as a guest of Benny Leonard, to attend *The Romance of a People*.

3

"Back on Independence Boulevard, I was cock of the walk," Ross later wrote. He was the biggest sporting star Chicago had produced in years, suddenly an exceedingly rich twenty-four-year-old. His take from the Canzoneri fight was $35,000, and in the months after the fight, he took in tens of thousands more in endorsements and appearances and testimonials. (Babe Ruth, the highest-paid player in baseball, peaked in 1931 with a two-year contract paying him

$80,000 annually.) It made for a dangerous brew: the adulation and thick wads of cash, the seemingly bottomless days between fights, killing time until he could go to the Chez Paree or the Haymarket joints. Outwardly, he had earned a reputation for being as clever in his business dealings as he was with his ring craft; he seemed that anomaly among young prizefighters of his time—a boy with a long-range plan. One Chicago columnist of the era foresaw that Barney was tracing a near-perfect trajectory—"hardly a misstep in his advancement"—and that he was one in a thousand fighters:

The dapper champion and his managers, Sam Pian and Art Winch, coming out of the Illinois State Boxing Commission office.

The career of Barney Ross is going to cheer and encourage a lot of youths less talented—and charmed. Just when most of us decide to agree that there positively is no other shortcut in the tough old fight game except the one leading down, always along comes someone like Barney Ross and gives us a laugh.

But we can almost sense the self-destructive impulse in those early-thirties photos of Ross with his fedora rakishly tilted over his thick-knit eyebrows, the boyish gap in his smile; the naivety that had him constantly falling prey to false friends, sycophants, and con artists hitting him up for loans and investments in harebrained business schemes. Ross was by nature a compulsive personality, with a weakness for alcohol, cigarettes, and women—but worst of all, he developed a pathological addiction to gambling.

Since the repeal of Prohibition earlier that year, gambling had been the Mob's most lucrative racket. Bookmaking joints were everywhere in Chicago, fronted by candy stores and pool halls, open secrets on every block. Ross tells us that he'd been introduced to the sport of horseracing by Al Jolson, who took him to Arlington Park northwest of Chicago. Before long, he became a fixture at Arlington; at Hawthorne and Sportsman's Park, two Capone-controlled racetracks in Cicero; at Jamaica and Belmont in New York; at Hialeah in Florida; and at Santa Anita in California.

Throughout his adult life, horseracing was the only spectator sport he truly took pleasure in—when he wasn't in the ring, he didn't enjoy attending prizefights—but he was a woeful gambler, took tips from anyone: stableboys, clockers, jockeys, bookies, even Louis B. Mayer, who owned a horse-racing stable. His bad luck at the track became legendary. He would almost never pick a winner. He was such a dreadful handicapper that, as he later recalled, Jolson refused to sit near him at the racetrack, telling the fighter: "Stay away from me—I don't want to catch your poison."

Ross was the polar opposite of betting geniuses like Arnold Rothstein, the New York–born organized-crime czar who had tutored the likes of Meyer Lansky, Charles "Lucky" Luciano, and Louis "Lepke" Buchalter, and who

Ross at his most beloved haunt, the racetrack.

enlisted the former featherweight champ Abe "the Little Hebrew" Attell to fix the 1919 World Series. Even the Yiddish *Forward* had once written admiringly of the breed of Jewish professional gamblers like Rothstein for being "clever and calculating, with iron wills and steel nerves."

But in his betting life, Barney Ross was anything but "iron-willed." He was the sort of sucker on whom the professional gamblers depended for their livelihood. In the height of his championship years, he was to become such a self-destructive gambler that Pian and Winch enlisted Barney's youngest brother as a spy. His brother George recalls how, at the age of seventeen, he'd been working as Barney's personal valet, in charge of seeing that all the champion's suits were cleaned, the sleeves hand-rolled, the shoes polished to a mirror shine; and he'd been instructed by Pian and Winch to check all the vest pockets for racing slips, reporting back on values of all the "losers." "But Barney was smarter than Pi and Winch. He started leaving ten or twenty-dollar losing slips in the pocket, and tore up the really big ones, the ones for $10,000 or more."

After beating Bobby Pacho in Los Angeles, March 27, 1934, Ross went out with some Hollywood friends and blew his entire purse—less the manager's third, of course—in one day's losing bets. "My credit was good with every bookie in the country," he later said, "but I could no longer cover my losses." He told Pian and Winch that he needed another blockbuster bout just to get himself out of the hole.

PART THREE

1

Barney's triumph over Tony Canzoneri would leave its mark on Chicagoans and New Yorkers for decades to come—even in the rarefied world of America's literati. According to Saul Bellow biographer James Atlas, the great novelist traveled east to New York in the 1940s and reminded William Barrett, an editor of the *Partisan Review*, of scrappy, fearless Barney Ross in his unprecedented conquest of the lightweight and welterweight boxing divisions. Like Ross, Barrett recalled, Bellow was "the kid from Chicago, carrying a chip on his shoulder ... ready to show these Eastern slickers that he was just as street-smart . . . as they were."

By the spring of 1934, Ross had so thoroughly dominated his division that there was no longer a big-money fight for him to make among the lightweight class. He had twice beaten Billy Petrolle, considered one of the best fighters never to win a championship belt; indeed, his domination of Petrolle in the Bronx Coliseum, perhaps the most skillful performance of Barney's career, would soon drive the Fargo Express into retirement. Ross knew he would have to step up in weight and take on the king of the welters, Jimmy "the Babyfaced Assassin" McLarnin.

McLarnin, considered the sport's hardest puncher outside the heavyweight division, had won the welterweight belt by demolishing Young Corbett III in a one-round knockout after Corbett had won the title from Barney's old friend and stablemate Jackie Fields. The signing of the contracts, after much public wrangling, created a frenzy in the sports pages.

"Greatest stir in many years of pugilistic history is created by the signing of Barney Ross, lightweight champion, and Jimmy McLarnin, welterweight champion," wrote Damon Runyon in the *Chicago Herald-American*. "This match is a ringworm's dream that few expected to see realized. . . . Ross is undoubtedly the greatest lightweight since Benny Leonard, last of the lightweight champions to make a bid for the welterweight title. McLarnin is one of the all-time ring stars. . . . A dynamite puncher [who] has for some years been feasting on fighters smaller than himself. But most of them were in terror of him before they entered the ring. No china chin, chicken heart awaits him when he faces the lathy, swift-moving boy from Chicago. . . . It looks as if the little fellows may at last be thoroughly avenged."

In New York City, as the *Toronto Globe and Mail* later reported, "McLarnin was the toast of Broadway, hobnobbing with Mayor Jimmy Walker, teaching Babe Ruth to box over drinks at Dinty Moore's and eating a slice of lemon pie with gangster Legs Diamond." In addition to the "Baby-

faced Assassin," the "Irish Lullaby" and the "Beltin' Celt,"
he had become known as the "Jew Beater," "Jewish Neme-
sis," the "Scourge of the Fighting Sons of Israel," owing to
his having dispatched in relatively short order Kid Kaplan,
Ruby Goldstein, Al Singer, Joe Glick, Joey Sangor, Jackie
Fields, and Sid Terris.

And for Jewish fight fans, the ultimate indignity came
when McLarnin knocked out the most revered of all modern
Jewish pugilists, the "ring-wizard," Benny Leonard himself.
Leonard, at thirty-six years old, seven years into his retirement, his prizefighting fortune lost in the stock-market
crash of 1929, decided to make an ill-advised comeback. He
was a shell of his former self, balding and paunchy and
scarcely the wizard of old, but he'd still managed to string
together nineteen wins and one draw when he signed to fight
the Babyfaced Assassin. "One of the reasons I want to lick
McLarnin is that I want to wipe out his successful record
against Jewish fighters," he said. In his prime, he might even
have accomplished it.

But Jimmy McLarnin, too young, too strong, had in the
sixth round knocked Benny Leonard unconscious. Even
McLarnin, it was widely reported, felt bad about the drub-
bing he had been forced to give this once most masterful of
scientific boxers; he candidly admitted some relief that
Benny wasn't a few years younger. It was to be the last fight
of Benny Leonard's astonishing career. "The real Leonard
already is immortal," wrote the *New York World-Telegram*,
"the artist of the ring canvas who glided up and back, the

genius of punch-slipping, the counter-puncher of lightning-reflex snap, the lion-hearted campaigner and the devoted believer in all that's good in boxing."

The loss stung the hearts of Jewish fans who'd always seen Benny Leonard as much more than a prizefighter. In the apocrypha that built up around him, Leonard had become a slick-haired superman of the ghetto streets, said to have once routed a pack of ruffians who were menacing an old Jewish woman and to have single-handedly waded into a mob of anti-Semites who were on the verge of defacing a synagogue on the Lower East Side.

It now fell on the slender shoulders of Dov-Ber Rasofsky to uphold the tradition of the Fighting Sons of Israel. After Pian and Winch had signed for the title bout with Pop Foster, McLarnin's English-born manager, a columnist in *The Ring* wrote: "It seems that the Jewish race stands a better chance than ever to avenge the K.O.'s administered to its boys, although I think that Barney has bitten off more than he can chew and will be taken into camp by the Fighting Irishman."

2

B arney Ross now ranked, alongside the Detroit Tigers' slugger Hank Greenberg, as the most admired Jewish athlete in the country. Far more than Benny Leonard ever had, Ross did not shy from his Orthodox background. He had taken to again wearing *tzitzis* under his custom-made suits, and wrapped phylacteries around his arm and placed them on his head during training camp. He was even seen with his late father's collection of religious books, poring over the pages of a Chumash and a Gemorrah.

The reporters couldn't help but notice; Pian and Winch tried to squash the Talmudic scholar story—everyone remembering what had transpired when Gene Tunney had been spotted by an Associated Press reporter trying to kill the dead training-camp hours before the Dempsey fight reading *A Winter's Tale*, *Hamlet*, and *Macbeth* and was subsequently mocked mercilessly as "Tunney, the great Shakesperean." Ross's managers feared that New York sportswriters would try to paint Barney as some Yeshiva-trained "fancy Dan" who would be murdered by a truly two-fisted pug like the Babyfaced Assassin. But Barney insisted he was honoring his father's memory; in a famous United Press photograph, snapped just days before the first McLarnin fight, he is shown with a small jeweled mezuzah attached by a chain to his belt loop. ("The 'charm' is a Mezuzah which carries a scroll from the Talmud," reads the caption.)*

Barney's training camp, once a near-monastic retreat of woodcutting, rope-jumping, and shadowboxing at Round Lake, Illinois, or the forests of Wisconsin, had now moved to the Grossinger's Resort in Ferndale, New York, and become

*This news caption is inaccurate: the mezuzah scroll carries two paragraphs from Deuteronomy 6, including the Sh'ma Yisroel.

a kind of Borscht Belt carnival, what with shadowboxing and Haftorah study mixed with games of pinochle and hours of vaudevillian clowning. Barney was the first professional fighter to train in the Catskills, but this spawned its own kind of championship lineage—Rocky Marciano, twenty years later, set up training camp in Grossinger's as did Ingemar Johansson and Floyd Patterson. Barney traveled from Chicago with a picaresque retinue, including a Chicago police officer named O'Connell on furlough to act as his bodyguard, and Mickey "Soldier" Farr, leader of the so-called Randolph Street Rovers, acting as official training-camp manager. Even the wisecracking barber, Harry Gelbart—whose son Larry would go on to fame as a screenwriter and creator of the TV show *M*A*S*H*—had closed up his Maxwell Street barbershop in order to give the champion daily hot-towel shaves while trading ribald Yiddish stories. Many of the leading stars of Broadway drove up to Grossinger's to watch him sparring: Al Jolson, Eddie Cantor, George Jessel, Fanny Brice.

And the sportswriters—in the most glamorous age of that profession—Damon Runyon, Grantland Rice, Jimmy Cannon, Red Smith, jotted down every detail of the lightweight champ's roadwork, his hundreds of sit-ups, the damage he was inflicting on his sparring partners (Barney apologizing when he dazed one; Art Winch yelling, "What the hell are you saying *sorry* for? *Hit* him!"), the extra plates of Jennie Grossinger's brisket and kasha he was stuffing down trying to add heft to his skinny frame. The columnists peppered Barney about how he felt giving away "eight or ten pounds to a tough cookie like Mac." When the writers kept talking about the not insubstantial weight difference, Ross recalled telling them, "Look, when I was fighting street fights in the gutters of the ghetto, I beat guys who outweighed me by forty pounds." The sportswriters told Ross that he wasn't facing the Babyfaced Assassin in a street fight.

3

It was that rare sporting event that leaps from the sports section to the front pages, reported alongside the massive Dustbowl storm—that cloud some 1,500 miles long and 2 miles high sweeping across the Great Plains—and the hail of Browning Automatic Rifle gunfire that killed Bonnie and Clyde in Louisiana. But in his Grossinger's retreat, Barney and his entourage talked mostly about the grim news out of Germany: the boycotts of Jewish businesses; Nazi-inspired pogroms in Poland; the reemergence of medieval libels—on May 1, *Der Stürmer* published a special issue which reminded readers that Jews had been charged with using the blood of Christian children in the Passover matzoh. Even the streets of New York City were roiling with Nazi activity, and not just in traditional German neighborhoods like Yorkville. On May 17, eleven days before the fight, a rally of 20,000 bearing swastika standards, goose-stepping in shiny black boots, and shouting "*Sieg Heil!*" filled Madison Square Garden for their "Pro-American Celebration of George Washington's Birthday." The rally had to be surrounded by an army of 1,700 police—then described as the largest antiriot squad in NYPD history—to fend off a surging crowd of anti-Nazi demonstrators in the streets outside the Garden, a mob that some press estimates put at 80,000.

In his training camp at Grossinger's, Barney boxed with a passion he had never felt before, hit the sandbag until it practically groaned, and said that the news from Germany had filled him with a new sort of resolve that made him feel "like I was fighting for all my people."

4

The trilogy stands alone in the annals of prizefighting: never in boxing history have two such highly skilled fighters faced each other in three world championship bouts, all staged within the span of one calendar year. From a promotional aspect we can see now the almost perfect symmetry of the pairing: just as Barney Ross had come to embody the essence of the scientific Jewish boxer, Jimmy Mc-Larnin—ramrod straight back, jutting chin, fierce blue eyes, with a golden harp embroidered on his bright green robe and a shamrock on his trunks—had become, in the words of one *Ring* columnist, "an absolute godlike idol with the Irish."

Their first fight was held May 28, 1934, in the Madison Square Garden Bowl in Long Island City, promoted as a benefit for Mrs. William Randolph Hearst's Free Milk Fund for Babies, Inc., and the gate of $210,000 was considered a small marvel given the bleak boxing economics of the Depression years. The side streets outside the Bowl were filled with men hawking glossy black-and-white photos of McLarnin and Ross, bags of peanuts four-for-a-dime, packs of cigarettes and chewing gum, and small rubber mats for fans to place on the hard wooden benches. The official attendance was listed as 60,000, the largest crowd for a nonheavyweight fight since the epic Benny Leonard–Lew Tendler bouts of 1922 and '23. The ringside dignitaries included Mayor Fiorello LaGuardia; the three New York baseball magnates—Charles Stoneham, Colonel Jacob Ruppert, Judge Stephen McKeever, owners of the Giants, Yankees, and Dodgers, respectively; the Marx Brothers; Jack Dempsey; Gene Tunney; Benny Leonard—wearing "a gay blue hat," noted one reporter—who sat ringside cheering for Ross to accomplish what he'd been unable to in challenging as a lightweight for Jack Britton's welterweight title. Also seated a few feet from press row was Father Charles E. Coughlin, described as "the celebrated radio speaker from Detroit" whose broadcasts, heard by an estimated 30 million listeners weekly, still had a populist pro–New Deal slant but would soon descend into vicious, anti-Semitic diatribes about the nefarious power of the "International Jew."

McLarnin danced into the ring in his meadow-green satin, and there was a long delay before Ross made his way down the aisle, half-sprinting with impatience in that tattered terrycloth robe—a standing joke now in the boxing community, the way Ma Rasofsky had been stitching and patching just to keep it a single, solid garment. Art Winch had to grab him by the arm and tell him to slow down, to wave to his fans; the referee wouldn't start the fight without him. Ross had never felt so tightly wound before a bout: this wasn't the usual prefight butterflies. He knew that tonight's action meant something more than a fifteen-rounder for the welterweight championship, that for Jews around the globe the glowing-white square of canvas had been transformed into something larger. One columnist had written before the fight that the reason so many Jewish boxers had lost to McLarnin was because, *as Jews*, they lacked the true fighting man's spirit. As Ross made his entrance, nodding to Benny Leonard in his royal-blue fedora, stepping up to the ring apron to return the Babyfaced Assassin's glare, he might have sensed around him the presence of Daniel Mendoza and Dutch Sam, Joe Choynski and Leach Cross, Ruby Goldstein and Battling Levinsky, and Abe Attell and Jackie Fields. . . .

Thirty years after the poet Bialik, in response to the Kishinev massacres, had asked, "Where are the heirs of the Hasmoneans?" in Jewish homes around the world, a fight had taken on the aspect of an allegory. Author Harold Ribalow, in *The Jew in American Sports*, recalls living in a neighborhood filled with ultra-Orthodox yeshiva students.

These boys knew little about boxing, but they could not miss the excitement throughout the city. And the fact that McLarnin had beaten many Jewish fighters made the event even more important to them. It was odd, watching these boys, with skullcaps on their heads, taking time out from their Talmudic studies to listen to a fight on the radio. And no matter how long I shall remember the famous trio of Ross-McLarnin fights, I shall recall the intense faces of the Jewish students who listened to each blow-by-blow account as though it were the most significant thing in the world.

There was no doubt that Ross could outdance McLarnin, but Barney's strategy was one of naked psychological warfare: to stand and trade with Babyface; to show he wasn't afraid of the big right hand. It was said that many of McLarnin's previous Jewish victims, like Al "the Bronx Beauty" Singer, had lost while still in the dressing room, so overwhelmed were they at the prospect of the knockout power in McLarnin's straight right.

The battle, as the front page of the next morning's *New York Times* reported, was "bitterly, systematically and, at times, savagely waged." In the first round the two fighters jabbed and hooked cautiously at long range. In the second, they clashed like bighorns, pounding relentlessly and clinching in the center of the ring. McLarnin hurt Ross with a right to the head, but Barney steadied himself and came back with a hissing left-right combination just before the bell to steal the round. He was now, in the view of one ringside reporter, "fierce as a dog lapping for action, cunning as a savage pitted against the wilderness." A clear pattern was established: Barney fighting in his typical savvy flurries,

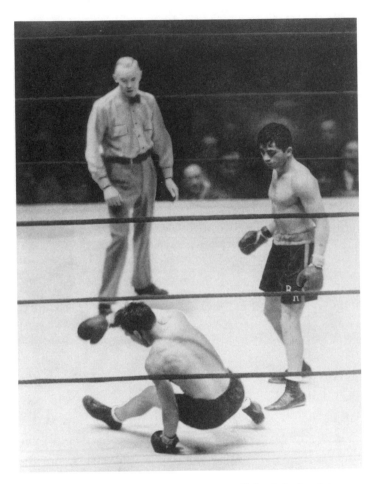

Ross stuns welterweight champion Jimmy "The Babyfaced Assassin" McLarnin in the ninth round, en route to his historic "triple-crown" victory in the Madison Square Garden Bowl, May 28, 1934.

conserving his energy, scoring frequently just before the bell, impressing the judges and taking the round. But in the ninth, McLarnin saw an opening, landing a short left hook that sent Ross to the canvas. He sprung up before the referee could even commence to count: "No one had ever counted over me in a prize ring and I wasn't about to let them start now," he recalled.

Twenty seconds later it was Barney's right hand that sent McLarnin to the canvas, and he too was back on his feet before a count could begin. They touched gloves sportingly before commencing the fifteenth round and in short order were standing toe-to-toe in the middle of the ring, swinging from the hip bone, then collapsing into exhausted clinches, only to continue digging fists again to the ribs and kidneys and solar plexus. Fatigue had overtaken science; this was little more than the wild slugging that had dominated mano a mano contests from the time of Cro-Magnon until the ascendance of Daniel Mendoza. In the final seconds Ross buckled McLarnin's knees with a clean shot just below the heart. McLarnin was trying desperately to land the heavy right hand, but Ross blocked or slipped all the punches and kept pounding Babyface hard with his own right hand at the bell.

Grabbing the overhead microphone, Joe Humphries began the announcement—"the winner and new welter-weight champion of the world"—but, drowned out by the roar in the Madison Square Garden Bowl, never got a chance to say the name Barney Ross. The "frail-waisted champion," the "raven-eyed Jew kid" was now the first fighter in history

His face swollen and bruised from the
previous night's work, Ross reads about
his exploits in his New York hotel suite.

to hold the lightweight and welterweight belts simultaneously. His youngest brother, George, was the first of the
ringside fans into Barney's corner, hugging him, seeing the
tears mixed with blood trickling down those ruddy cheeks.
"This fight meant so much to me—if I'd lost it, I'd have
died."

The sportswriters in press row left no record of what
Father Charles Coughlin said upon seeing the Jewish
fighter's fist raised overhead.

5

The hero's welcome was organized by Alderman Jack Arvey, formerly of Maxwell Street, now the powerful Democratic fixer in the 24th Ward—the predominantly Jewish district that Franklin Roosevelt in 1933 had called "the best Democratic ward in the country"—and the champion's imminent arrival on the Broadway Limited was trumpeted for days in advance. "He came home today," Gene Morgan wrote breathlessly in the *Chicago Daily News*, "home to the arms of his adoring Chicago—Barney Ross, thrice-crowned emperor of fistdom, whose Alexander-the-Greatness has won him three fighting titles within a year. . . . It was a welcome such as only Chicago can tender to a native son who has added to the city's achievement in science, literature, music or jaw-busting."

When the train pulled into Union Station at 9:45 a.m. on Monday, June 4, he was met by his mother and brothers, and rode through the swarming streets in an open touring car, dressed in a grey-striped sack suit, his necktie a "symphony of gray and blue," waving a green felt fedora at the crowd. His mother clutched two dozen roses, as they followed the wailing police sirens down Jackson Boulevard to LaSalle Street, pelted by tons of ticker tape, arriving at their homecoming rally at City Hall. A forty-piece band played "Chicago," and Barney wryly told the crowd that, yes, he had beaten a beloved Irish-born champion of the world, been

escorted from Union Station by a hundred Chicago policemen with the map of Ireland written all over their faces, and
been given a civic blessing by a mayor with the grand name
of Kelly. "The Irish are the greatest of sportsmen. I'm
almost ashamed I licked one."

With the victory champagne still flowing in the Morrison
Hotel, negotiations were on for McLarnin-Ross II, again to
be held at Long Island City's Madison Square Garden Bowl.
The fight was delayed by rain, and then by Rosh Hashanah,
because Ross steadfastly refused to fight or train during the
High Holy Days, then finally rescheduled for September 17,
1934. What a heady late-summer moment it must have been
for American Jews. The Detroit Tigers' Hank Greenberg

Holder of three world titles, Ross returns to his
hometown and is given a hero's welcome. He sits with
his mother and Chicago alderman Jack Arvey during the
parade down La Salle Street.

was, almost simultaneously, making his own bold statement as a public Jewish athlete. On September 10, 1934, Greenberg decided to play in a late-season game against the Boston Red Sox, despite the fact that it was Rosh Hashanah. He hit two solo home runs in a 2-to-1 Tigers victory. Before the game, reporters had sought out rabbinical opinions, with the *Detroit News* running the headline TALMUD CLEARS GREENBERG FOR HOLIDAY PLAY. "The team was fighting for first place, and I was probably the only batter in the lineup who was not in a slump," the majestic slugger recalled. "But in the Jewish religion, it is traditional that one observe[s] the holiday solemnly, with prayer. . . . I wasn't sure what to do."

On September 19, with the Tigers slated to play the New York Yankees on Yom Kippur, Greenberg refused to suit up, putting his identity as a Jew before his identity as a professional athlete. In the *Detroit Free Press*, an Edgar Guest poem celebrated Greenberg:

> Came Yom Kippur—holy fast day world wide over to
> the Jew,
> And Hank Greenberg to his teaching and the old
> tradition true
> Spent the day among his people and he didn't come to
> play.
> Said Murphy to Mulrooney, "We shall lose the game
> today!
> We shall miss him on the infield and shall miss him at
> the bat

But he's true to his religion—and I honor him for that!"

6

As the champion, Barney Ross came into the second McLarnin bout an 11-to-5 favorite, 6 pounds lighter than his Irish-Canadian rival. It was another close-quarters battle, with the two men, having adjusted to the other's strategies, fighting with reversed tactics: McLarnin relying more on his jab and short left hooks to the head and body, while Ross was prepared to trade, throwing frequent heavy right-hand punches to Jimmy's chin and rib cage. "[Barney] actually outpunched the famous hitter, McLarnin, no matter what the judging officials thought about it," wrote Nat Fleischer in *The Ring*. McLarnin's left eye was swollen shut by the fight's end, and he looked the beaten man, but the decision was split in favor of the former newsboy from Vancouver. Twenty-two of the twenty-eight sportwriters covering the bout disagreed with the verdict, scoring a Ross victory. The fact that McLarnin, both judges, and the referee were all of Irish descent wasn't lost on many of the crowd, and a joke began to circulate even as the crowd was streaming out of the Bowl: *Did you hear the one about the four Irishmen and the Jew?*

The split in the first two fights set up the decisive rubber match, a third world welterweight championship—Barney having since willingly abdicated his lightweight belt—

scheduled for May 28, 1935, the one-year anniversary of the first McLarnin-Ross fight. It was staged in the Polo Grounds in front of 45,000 fans, and refereed by Jack Dempsey; this time, Pian and Winch had negotiated for a Jewish official named Abe Goldberg to be placed in one of the judges' seats. On an unseasonably warm and humid night, the ringside seats at Coogan's Bluff were filled with "shirtsleeved notables" such as Yankee star Lou Gehrig and a then up-and-coming Detroit heavyweight named Joe Louis, who was introduced to the crowd in his first-ever appearance in a New York prize ring.

Many observers considered it the most thrilling fight of the trilogy; from the outset Ross was the quicker and more aggressive fighter, staggering McLarnin on several occasions, consistently beating him to the punch. As Henry McLemore, the United Press correspondent, rendered it:

> For fifteen rounds at the Polo Grounds last night McLarnin, once again the babyfaced bomber, threw every punch he had, executed every wile learned in years and years of fighting the best of 'em. But it wasn't enough. When the boys came out for the twelfth it was anybody's fight, and you knew that the title, and the gold and the glory that goes with it, rested on what happened from there out. Ross, despite breaking a bone in his left hand in the sixth round, went out for it. He took the twelfth with a left to the stomach that popped McLarnin's mouth open and bent him double.

The judges and referee Jack Dempsey were unanimous in their scoring: a clear-cut victory for Barney Ross. Wrote Jimmy Powers in his New York *Daily News* column: "Ross has won permanent possession of McLarnin." And Damon Runyon, in the *New York American:* "In the most desperate fifteen-round fight between little men that has been seen in many a year . . . [the fighting] was so fierce and so close, every step of the journey, with the men fighting half the time head-to-head."

In the grainy newsreel footage of the fight, Ross and McLarnin can be seen slugging furiously in the final seconds of the fifteenth, Jimmy desperate for a last-ditch knockout, Barney feverishly responding, wanting to leave no doubt in the judges' scorecards. And then the bloodied gladiators fall into a final clinch, half-collapsing with arms around each other's shoulders, as a hundred flashbulbs burst, two superbly trained athletes in their prime—Barney at age twenty-six, Jimmy at thirty-one—knowing that they will be forever linked in this moment. Babyface waltzes with Barney toward Art Winch and Izzy Kline, who are waiting to mop up the sweat and wrap the Pride of the Ghetto in his terry-cloth stripes. Barney stands awaiting the verdict, white towel draped over his head like a prayer shawl. Jimmy turns, like a playground prankster, summoning a final burst of adrenaline, and does a crazed cartwheel and somersault back to his own corner.

Jimmy McLarnin was that rarity among professional boxers, retiring with both his wits and his fortune (in addition to his carefully invested winnings, his manager and surrogate father, Pop Foster, had left McLarnin everything in his will); he settled in Southern California where, a scratch golfer, he spent long afternoons on manicured greens with friends like Bob Hope, Bing Crosby, and Humphrey Bogart. He outlived all of them—even Hope—outlived Ross by more than thirty years, and spent his final days a half-forgotten champion, living a quiet life into his late nineties in Washington State, near his children and grandchildren. He remains the last link in the great chain of Irish world champions, a name still invoked with reverence by old-school fight aficionados, a faded photograph framed in saloons from Belfast to Hell's Kitchen.

Decades later, all acrimony had faded; for the remainder of Barney's life, he and Jimmy were fast friends, sending each other holiday cards and birthday wishes. From the vantage point of post–World War II America, McLarnin wistfully confessed that he had always hated the sobriquets "Hebrew Scourge" and "Jew Beater."

PART FOUR

1

For Barney Ross, it should have ended there, in that perfect frozen flashbulb waltz. Getting the best of the Baby-faced Assassin would have been the capstone to a glorious career. But he soldiered on, fighting with a frequency unthinkable today—taking on three top-flight contenders in the course of a summer. He had his mother and younger brothers to support, the bloated entourage—growing larger with every fight, it seemed—and headstrong Barney had never listened to Jackie Fields's warning to watch for the bloodsuckers in his midst. And then there was his insatiable gambler's itch; he was constantly bleeding more money to bookmakers and at racetrack windows than he could ever hope to make in the ring.

As a defensive boxer, he still had no peer among his contemporaries, and for that reason he had yet to be badly injured in a fight. But late in 1935, when Ross fought the tough Filipino welterweight contender Ceferino Garcia, there were intimations of the devastation Henry Armstrong would later inflict. In their first of three bouts, a ten-rounder in San Francisco, Garcia's looping "bolo" punch flattened Barney twice in one round. He stumbled back to his corner, and, in at least one telling of the tale, Art Winch struck a match, holding the flame to Barney's bare back to get the fighter to respond to the standard questions. "What round is it?" Barney stared mutely into his spit pail. "End of the first," he said at long last. "Barn, it's the fifth." Fighting on street instinct and sheer muscle memory, Barney hung in for a decision, but his face and body were battered. He would beat the strapping Filipino twice more in the next two years, and then he punched a clear path through a string of lesser challengers, knocking out the likes of Lou Halper, Henry "Chuck" Woods, Laddie Tonelli, Morrie Sherman, decisioning Izzy Jannazzo during Mike Jacobs's Madison Square Garden "Tournament of Champions," the first time five world championships had ever been staged on one fight card.

Perhaps it was becoming too easy, the competition barely testing his limits. Even his once-relentless training regimen was slackening; he could sneak a few puffs of a Chesterfield in the middle of a gym workout, pass the butt to his kid brother George, who would take the withering lecture from Art Winch when he smelled the smoke in the rubdown room. He was drinking straight vodka at night because it left less of a trace on the breath the next morning. He was at the peak of his prizefighting prowess but already dreading the boredom that would come with retirement. What would he do as an ex-champ? Fasten a referee's bow tie like Benny Leonard, Abe Attell, and Ruby Goldstein? Manage his own fighting stable? He was already handling Davey Day, a promising Jewish lightweight from the West Side. He invested in a jewelry store in downtown Chicago, took an executive's title there, even appeared in the Chicago papers with a jeweler's loupe screwed into his eye socket, as if counting carats might actually be a plausible postfight career.

He met his first wife, Pearl Siegel, while in training camp at Grossinger's. She was a petite, cherub-cheeked New York girl, daughter of a prominent manufacturer of women's clothing. They were married on December 5, 1937, at the Congress Hotel in Chicago—Barney signing the marriage license under the name his brothers were using, Rasof—and were photographed, Pearl in a pillbox hat, Barney with his right hand shoved into the pocket of a tweed three-piece suit, on the deck of a luxury liner bound for a European honeymoon.

Upon returning to New York, the couple set up a fashionable residence in the Century Apartments, the 1931 Art Deco building on Central Park West. But for Barney, the orphan who fought his way to respectability, the concept "home" was always somehow beyond his grasp. In a guest column he wrote in the *New York Evening Post* on the eve of one of his championship bouts, Ross describes his inability to ever truly settle down in conventional domesticity.

My lack of plans is the only thing my wife has complained about. I honestly don't know whether I will make my home in Chicago or in New York. Mrs. Ross found a furnished apartment in New York the other day, but I told her I thought we should get an unfurnished one, furnish it and settle down. She threw up

Mr. and Mrs. Barney Ross (née Pearl Siegel), and Miss Barbara
Teps (right), at the opening of the Casa Mañana, Billy Rose's new
nightclub in New York City, January 19, 1938. (© *Bettmann*/CORBIS)

her hands and suggested that I make up my mind what part of the United States we were going to live in. . . . I'm by nature restless and I always want to be going somewhere. People tell me that my success in the ring has been due to my restless energy. I suspect they're right. I would never be able to train at an isolated training camp. If I couldn't train at a place such as the Grossinger's Country Club, I'd prefer to work in a city gymnasium. . . .

In those mid-thirties championship years, he seems like the grasshopper in the Aesop fable, fiddling through late summer while his managers, Pian and Winch, and his fiscally shrewd older brother, Ben, keep warning him about the coming frost. His reputation for overtipping and loaning thousands to friends was now legendary beyond his old Roosevelt Road haunts. He celebrated his third win over Ceferino Garcia at Cicero's Washington Park racetrack, losing his entire $18,000 purse in a few hours, betting wrong on eight races out of eight.

There are hundreds of classic photographs of the champion in that comet-tail's glow, always in the immaculately cut suits, the silk pocket square, the gleaming jewelry. He sits shoulder-to-shoulder with J. Edgar Hoover in Harlem's Cotton Club in 1936, exchanging confidences—racing tips?—over cocktails and a pressed white tablecloth. Leaning on the white-picket railing of Churchill Downs with Jack Dempsey at the running of the 1936 Kentucky Derby. Holding court in Toots Shor's nightclub and at the grand opening

FBI director J. Edgar Hoover and Ross meet at the famed Cotton
Club in Harlem, November 30, 1936. (© *Bettmann*/CORBIS)

of producer Billy Rose's Casa Mañana. His brown eyes burning with the savage laughter of Oscar Wilde's aphorism:
"Moderation is a fatal thing; nothing succeeds like excess."
There is a widely published shot of Barney taken on the very
night that he won the last fight with McLarnin, standing in
the glare of an unnamed New York nightspot, broken hand
bandaged, face swollen like an eggplant, eyes reduced to
slits; and on each punch-weary arm hang a pair of platinum
blondes, four high-heeled Mae Wests in tight silk dresses
and mink stoles. In the *Chicago Daily News*, the photo ran
under the cutline TO THE VICTOR BELONGS THE GOILS.

Like the Golem—that mythic man of clay who was created by a kabbalist to save the Jewish people and winds up running amok—Ross became a prisoner of the very restless impulses that had catapulted him to boxing greatness.

2

I t's one of the many paradoxes of Barney Ross's career that the fight often cited as his bravest performance was also the worst beating he ever suffered in the ring. He'd been a professional boxer nearly a decade when, at age twenty-eight, he signed to fight Henry Armstrong, the relentlessly aggressive and superbly conditioned featherweight champion. Born Henry Jackson in 1912 in Columbus, Mississippi, on the very plantation where his grandmother had been a slave, Armstrong was a straightforward pressure fighter with knockout power in both hands. Defensive tactics weren't part of his arsenal, and his swarming windmill style, said to have been the blueprint for later punchers like Joe Frazier and the young Mike Tyson, earned him a host of monikers: Hurricane Henry, the Human Buzzsaw, Homicide Hank, Hammerin' Hank, Little Perpetual Motion. His most feared punch was known as "the blackout," a short looping right, neither hook nor cross but a flicking-fast blow to the chin. "It moved in a circular path, but only about ten inches," Armstrong recalled. "A terrible thing to do to anybody. Most of them never saw it coming."

Even today, his scorched-earth campaign leading up to the welterweight title fight with Barney Ross remains unparalleled: between January 1937 and March 1938, Armstrong won an astounding thirty-seven fights in a row, thirty-five by knockout. In one fearsome stretch he had knocked out twenty-seven straight opponents. Finally, from Petey Sarron, knocked out in six, he stripped the world featherweight championship's belt.

Still, it was nearly unthinkable that a fighter coming from the featherweights (the 126-pound limit) could leapfrog a full division and dethrone a supremely skilled boxer who had reigned undefeated at 147 pounds for more than three years. Barney Ross was installed by oddsmakers as the 5-to-2 favorite, with most of the experts citing the old fistic truism that a "good big man will always beat a good little man."

In the prefight promotion, some sportswriters tried to overplay their typical ethnic rivalry stories; because Barney had fought only a relatively few black fighters, and because the two armed robbers who'd murdered his father on Jefferson Street had been black, some tried to say that Barney had a "colored" problem, had developed a special hatred for African-American fighters. It was ludicrous, as even a casual sports fan would have known: Barney Ross was often seen in the company of his close friend Joe Louis. The articles angered Barney; he had Pi and Winch escort one magazine writer out of the Grossinger's training camp. Henry Armstrong, who once said, "You can't Jim Crow a left hook," was writing poetry in his training camp at Pompton Lakes, New Jersey. Hugh Bradley, columnist for the *New York Post*, ran one of Armstrong's poems—"In Contemplation of May 26," jotted in the fighter's own cramped handwriting—on the front page of the May 24 sports section.

> Two fighters of oppressed races fighting each other,
>   just like that
> It doesn't seem exactly sensible or right
> We're not mad at each other; we're just fighting for
>   the things we need
> It comes right back, the same old thing—to live, man
>   must fight

The bout was delayed three times by heavy rain. Barney was uncharacteristically irritable. A few nights before the fight, sitting with his brother George in the Edison Hotel in Manhattan, trying to kill the tense hours with some two-handed claviache, he played his cards badly and suddenly flung the entire deck in his kid brother's face, drawing blood from the chin. He apologized profusely. It didn't augur well.

The weather broke and the fight finally took place in the Madison Square Garden Bowl on May 31, 1938. Armstrong had been invited to the Pompton Lakes training camp of Joe Louis—the Brown Bomber, friendly with both the feather-weight and welterweight champs, was preparing for his now-legendary second fight with Max Schmeling that June. Gulping beer and gorging himself just to make the minimum weight for a welterweight bout, Armstrong managed to tip the scales at 133 pounds. Barney Ross came in 8½ pounds heavier, at 142. Barney stood an inch taller than the five-foot-five-inch Armstrong, and with his considerable reach advantage, it was thought he would be able to neutralize the Hurricane's relentless onslaught with a classic strategy of stiff jabbing and defensive sidestepping straight out of the Daniel Mendoza school.

Many boxing histories make the mistake of describing the fight as a "massacre," a mismatch from start to finish, as if Barney Ross was beaten from ring post to ring post for forty-five straight minutes. It might indeed have ended in a bloodbath, but it certainly didn't begin that way. Watching the newsreel footage of the bout recently, I could discern the prizefight that might have been: in the first and second rounds, Barney is clearly the sharper fighter, the master boxer, his crisp jab and crafty footwork keeping the charging, low-crouching Armstrong on his heels.

And then suddenly, after the fourth, the horrible Dorian Gray moment: the welterweight champion ages twenty years in a matter of seconds. Young Barney Ross is gone— the clever fighter who outfoxed the Fargo Express for ten rounds, who wrestled the championship belts from Tony Canzoneri and Jimmy McLarnin—replaced now by some leaden-legged, defenseless impostor, a mere husk. Armstrong, whose sixteen-inch neck and thick chest and back muscles make him look like a scale model of Joe Louis, bulls straight ahead, forehead permanently glued to Barney's collarbone. The savage infighting neutralizes Barney's jabbing. He has no option but to stand and slug.

The rest is a dreadful thing to watch, like hidden-camera footage of a baseball-bat beating. Barney could never quite explain the sudden paralysis in his legs: it was as if he'd taken a numbing needle at the base of his spine. Where was the gorgeous pivoting geometry of footwork? His leopard-like grace in slipping punches? As he stood toe-to-toe with the Human Buzzsaw, he had a vision of his own demise when the blackout punch floated in slow-motion to connect squarely with his jaw: "I had my left raised to strike and I saw that punch coming—and he hit me. Right away he hit me again with the same punch and then caught me with a hook. I knew then. I knew that if Armstrong could hit me with that punch, then I was through."

But he didn't quit. Round after round, he kept getting off the stool, only to stand immobile, now blind in one eye, blood-spattered, pawing pitifully with his left hand like a drunken man groping for a wall in the darkness. Armstrong's gloves were soaked from the hot streams flowing from Barney's smashed nose and mouth. The smaller man bobbing and crowding, double-hooking, Barney's neck jerking violently, his eyes shut, mouth agape—at moments he resembles nothing so much as Oswald shot in the belly by Jack Ruby in the Dallas police station. And the cries began to echo in the Bowl: "Stop it! For God's sake, stop it!" When Armstrong let go a murderous volley in the fourteenth, Barney's legs bent feebly—but still he didn't fall. With all ring craft and subterfuge evaporated, he was left with sheer will; Grantland Rice the next morning would write of "Barney Ross, game to the last drop of blood . . . fighting the last ten rounds on instinct and condition . . ."

The punishment was so relentless that Sam Pian said he had no choice but to throw in the towel. "Don't do it," Barney mumbled though swollen lips. "I'm not quitting. If you stop it, I'll never talk to you again." He wanted to surrender his title as he'd won it: on his feet, not slumped on a wooden stool.

Between the eleventh and twelfth rounds, referee Art Donovan crouched in the champion's corner. He was going to have to end the beating—it would be the first technical knockout of Barney's career.

"Let me finish," Ross said.

"You can't protect yourself."

"I'll never fight again after this one. I promise you that, if you let me finish."

Donovan nodded grimly and told the champ he'd better start throwing some punches. The jabs were perfunctory, the shuffling pitiful, yet it was enough—barely—to demonstrate signs of life behind the glazed eyes. In the center of that illuminated square the two men locked again in a kind of sadomasochistic tango. Barney never backing up, never ducking, his torso and skull absorbing the short hooks and uppercuts. After the fight, one writer calculated that Armstrong had thrown 1,200 punches. Perhaps Henry carried Barney the final four rounds out of respect—Armstrong later said he'd eased up on his power so that the once-great champion wouldn't suffer his first ever stoppage. If so, wrote sports columnist Milton Gross, "he carried Ross's body, not his heart." As Barney was led from the ring, his face a map of welts, Grantland Rice called out from press row: "Why didn't you quit? Did you want to get killed?"

"Champ's privilege. A champ's got the right to choose the way he goes out."

Many in the Bowl had gone mute; thick-necked men in fedoras were visibly crying. Ross later described his recollection of the moment: "I don't hear any shouting. I don't even hear talking. How come they're not raising the roof for the hero of the night, the new champ? I saw faces, faces, faces, and they were all looking at me, not up at the ring, and in the whole arena, 35,000 people were sitting in silence. And then I suddenly realized that this unbelievable, fantastic silence was the most wonderful tribute I had ever received. It spoke louder, a thousand times louder than all the cheers I had ever heard since the day I put on a pair of boxing gloves and won my first fight."

He had often told sportswriters like Rice and Runyon that he would only take one real beating. He wasn't going to go the route of so many fading champions, gradually diminishing in skill until they are pummeled by third-rate club fighters. He wasn't going to end up sleepy-eyed and rubber-tongued—what Slapsie Maxie Rosenbloom, in one of his stand-up routines, called "plain punch goofy." There was no shame in losing to Henry Armstrong, a future Hall of Famer; only two months later, beating lightweight champion Lou Ambers in a bloody slugging match (during which Armstrong was reported to have ingested over a quart of his own blood), the little Hurricane would trump Ross's earlier record, go into boxing annals as the first man in history to hold featherweight, lightweight, and welterweight belts simultaneously.

In his dressing room, awash in sweat and blood, face grotesquely battered, Ross announced his retirement from the ring. "That was my last fight. And I wasn't going to go out lying down. Armstrong is one hell of a fighter, but I would have got up had he knocked me down a dozen times." Many years later, during the Joe Louis–Ezzard Charles bout, he would find himself getting up from his ringside seat in Madison Square Garden, walking up the aisle in disgust. Asked by Milton Gross why he'd left, Ross said: "You don't want to see it when it's not there anymore. Watching Joe tonight I thought about myself against Henry Armstrong. I'd see an opening and when I tried to do something about it, it was gone. He was murdering me and I couldn't help myself. I finally said to myself, 'Beryleh, you're through. What are you doing in here?' "

With his solid fan base in New York and Chicago, he was still a matchmaker's dream; Mike Jacobs was already talking about promoting a third fight with Tony Canzoneri. But Barney declined all offers. He closed the door on his professional life as a boxer with a record of 74 wins, 4 losses, 3 draws. The most remarkable statistic of all: in nearly a decade as an amateur and professional, he had never been knocked out. His place in the prizefighting pantheon was ensured. In August 1938, when *The Ring* ran a series of photographs of Armstrong pummeling him in the later rounds, the rubric read DOWNFALL OF A TITAN.

PART FIVE

1

Barney Ross was hospitalized for days after the Armstrong fight, and on the long train ride back to Chicago, Harry the Barber had to keep applying hot towels so that by the time they arrived in Union Station, with a pair of dark glasses, he could face the world.

He tried to fashion a home with his wife, Pearl—first in New York and later in Chicago. The press came out to photograph his first day at work as a manager for Pearl's father's clothing company. But Barney's restive heart couldn't handle a desk job, certainly not one that had him overseeing the sales force in a fleet of women's ready-to-wear retail stores in New Jersey. He'd find himself back in the streets around Madison Square Garden, entertaining sportswriters in Stillman's Gym on 8th Avenue or inside Toots Schor's new restaurant on 51st Street, a "temple of sports celebrity" where he was still swarmed by well-wishers and fans when he entered the room.

The stories of his late-night carousing are legion. His father-in-law, who also lived in the Century, would "grease" the doormen with $5 to keep tabs on his wayward son-in-law.

Barney, the savvy son of Maxwell Street, would slip them a ten and the admonishment "You don't know when I got in."

Looking for another taste of the limelight, he dragged Pearl up to Grossinger's resort. He even tried acting in a Doc Leo Michel production of Clifford Odet's *Golden Boy* but quickly realized that delivering credible dialogue with trained actors was a far cry from trading jabs with Jimmy McLarnin.

Before long he drifted back to Chicago, managing a hotel tavern in the Loop for a few months before opening his own bar. In 1940, he opened the Barney Ross Cocktail Lounge at 5 North Clark Street, directly across the street from the Morrison Hotel. It was a nightspot modeled partly on the Toots Schor's formula: old prizefighters and baseball players rubbing shoulders with politicos and Outfit heavies. He had a piano player and a cabaret singer. On slower nights Barney would sit down at the keyboard himself and entertain his friends with the show tunes and Yiddish theater standards he played by ear. His brother Ben ran the business, while Barney put in time glad-handing the press and celebrity clientele.

Pearl knew, long before she filed for divorce, that the marriage was no good. On a long walk with George Rasof one night in Manhattan, she said, "Your brother, I adore him—I don't know how I'm going to live without him." By early 1942, their separation was fodder for Irv Kupcinet, the former college football star whose then-nascent gossip column was to become a Chicago institution for more than half a century: "Barney, in his straightforward manner, says his marriage was a mistake . . . that their widely separated temperaments made it advisable for them to part." Privately, Barney told his brother Ben that Pearl badly wanted to have children with him, but he'd long ago decided he could never really be a proper father.

2

And now the dark moods began to take hold. He would turn up at his youngest brother George's apartment at any hour of the night, wanting to walk in the rain, begging for companionship but no conversation. "C'mon, Yunk, let's walk," he'd say, then throw him a raincoat and hat and tramp from the 1300 block of Independence Boulevard several miles down to the Chicago Stadium, scene of so many of his old triumphs, never saying a word.

Ed Wynn, the rubber-faced comedian who'd got his start in the *Ziegfeld Follies*, introduced Ross to the dancer he was to marry, divorce, and marry again. Her name was Catherine Howlett. She had also got her start in the *Follies*, and she'd come to Chicago in 1940 to work as a chorus girl in Wynn's musical revue, *Boys and Girls Together*. Barney met Cathy backstage after a performance and was instantly smitten. She was a long, leggy brunette with the high cheekbones and soft eyes of Rita Hayworth. His divorce wasn't yet final when they began dating. Unlike the pampered Pearl Siegel, Cathy Howlett's background had more of Barney's rockiness; she'd had an early marriage and was the mother of a daughter, Noreen, who suffered from a rheumatic heart condition and was living with relatives on Long Island. After *Boys and Girls Together* finished up its Chicago run, she was supposed to continue on tour with Wynn, but Barney begged her to stay in Chicago with him. He asked a friend who managed the Chez Paree nightclub to get her a place dancing in the chorus nightly. After the divorce from Pearl was finalized, he asked Cathy to marry him.

The conventional version of his enlisting in the Marine Corps has Barney holding court in his cocktail lounge on North Clark Street, arguing with some sportswriters about how long his friend Joe Louis would reign as heavyweight champ, when the news of the Japanese attack on Pearl Harbor came. Immediately after hearing President Roosevelt's declaration of war, he decided he had to enlist in the Marines. In later writings, he said he was intent on seeing combat because he was the only one of the five Rasofsky boys who could serve. Ben was almost forty-five; Morrie had serious back trouble; Sam was discharged from the Navy after suffering an epileptic seizure; and George, with a history of ulcers and bad feet, had been rejected by the draft board. Barney walked into the Marine recruiting office in the Loop and was told that at nearly thirty-three he was too old to enlist. It took sixty days for him to get an age waiver from Washington. His mother collapsed when he told her. "*Gott gie mit dir,*" she said. Irv Kupcinet broke the news of Barney's enlistment as a buck private in his column of February 3, 1942. "I'm frank enough to admit that I don't like being a sol-

dier but our country needs men and that's where I belong,"
Ross said. "And in the front lines, not back teaching kids
how to box." He added, somewhat prophetically: "Don't
think I haven't dreamed of a few bullets coming my way."

3

I sensed that there was something a little more complex
than Barney Ross's love affair with Uncle Sam, some jagged
riddle resting in that smoke-filled interregnum between his
championship reign and the return to America as a decorated war hero, and in the spring of 2003, I made the first of
several pilgrimages to Chicago to interview Ross's last surviving brother.

Twice-widowed, the youngest of Barney's five siblings,
George Rasof was eighty-six and living alone in a small one-
bedroom apartment in a high-rise retirement community in
the village of Niles, so close to the O'Hare flight path that as
the jets boomed overhead in their unceasing descent, it felt
like we were sitting on an extension of a runway. I'd spoken
to George several times on the phone from New York, but
when I knocked at the door of his apartment in the Golf Mill
Estates—"independent living," he had stressed, when I'd
made the mistake of thinking it was a nursing home—I
wasn't sure quite what to expect. From the few descriptions
in Barney's autobiography, I still had images of a tiny boy,
perhaps eight or nine, galloping down the hallways of that

gloomy West Side orphanage in knickers and tweed cap to greet his big brother after he'd taken the world's lightweight belt from Tony Canzoneri.

He had the lean frame of a man who could have jockeyed thoroughbreds at Sportsman's Park, stood perhaps five feet three and weighed 121 pounds, with electric black eyes, bright white teeth, and white hair swept perfectly back. He greeted me with a handshake and half a hug like I was a wayward grandson.

He'd been a jeweler for many years. Around his neck he wore a gold Star of David that he had designed, fifty years earlier, for his mother. When Sarah Rasofsky died, the pendant went to George's sister, Ida Kaplan, and when Ida died, the Star of David made a return to its designer. In addition to working in the gold and diamond trade, he'd had a side career as a semiprofessional jazz trumpet player, and in his bedroom he kept an electric organ that he still enjoyed playing in the evening. He suffered from smoking-related emphysema and a raft of digestive problems, but, as I was to learn, he still regularly enjoyed nine holes of golf, a cold can of Bud Light on a Saturday night, and, like my father, suffered from that inexplicable fervor that leads thousands of North Siders each spring to don bright blue caps and believe that a miracle might happen this season on Addison Street.

"You got here just in time," he told me, though his meaning was less ominous than it first sounded. His sparsely furnished apartment was cluttered with suitcases, stacks of papers, cardboard boxes—all memorabilia from his big brother's boxing career, which he was in the slow process of parceling out to various family members: his daughter, Susie, in Atlanta; several nephews in the Chicago area. "Maybe someday my grandchildren will be curious, want to know who their uncle Barney really was," he told me.

To George the piles were just so much detritus; to me it was like I'd stumbled into Aladdin's cave. I spread clippings and original wire-service photos before me on the carpet: Barney with Joe Louis, whom George still judged to be the greatest heavyweight of them all ("Ali, I don't think would have lasted two rounds with Joe . . . Joe was so methodical"); Barney with Sugar Ray Robinson; Barney with Rocky Marciano; Barney with the buffoonish Maxwell Street heavyweight Kingfish Levinsky ("King was always missing a day of the week," George said, smiling.).

George had been a Golden Glove champion himself, winning the flyweight novice division in 1935 with his brother Barney working as his second. "In those days, you fought twice in the same night; if you won your first fight, you fought again. I boxed the nephew of Sammy Mandell, the former lightweight champion. I knocked the kid out. Then I had another fight that I won, then they had the semifinals and the finals the same night at the Chicago Stadium. Barney was working my corner. He said, 'Yunk, do you feel the sweat running down your armpits?' I said, 'Sure, I do.' 'That's good, I always did, too. Not out of fright, just nervousness. That'll keep you sharp.' "

Sam Pian and Art Winch told George he had the makings of a professional, but Ma Rasofsky had forbidden it. "She put her foot down. *Genug.* One was enough." Arch Ward had written up Barney's youngest brother as the lead item in his *Chicago Tribune* column, and George still had the brittle yellow original in those stacks of clippings:

> Mrs. Sarah Rasovsky, mother of Barney Ross, says she has a younger son who can punch the head off the world's lightweight, junior-welterweight and welterweight champion, but she will never consent to his fighting. . . .

I spent a long weekend in the glow of that wizened Golden Glover, and when I came back a few months later for another interview, the stacks of wire-service photos and clippings had shifted around the room like so many rooks and bishops, but nothing seemed to have been sent yet to his daughter's house in Atlanta. Almost everyone in the Golf Mill Estates now assumed that I was George's grandson, and it became too tiresome to keep making rote corrections. "He's my biographer," George joked one afternoon as we got out of the elevator in the lobby. We drove in my rented Grand Am to his favorite Chinese restaurant, the China Chef in Morton Grove, listening to the AM radio broadcast of the Cubs playing the Sox in a summertime interleague series. The game was rain-delayed, a torrent falling on the South Side, though it was still bright blue skies for us up in north Chicagoland. It took thirty minutes for the violent thunderstorm to drift over us, and then it began to pour so hard I couldn't see the road in front of me. In the China Chef, over shrimp and fried rice, George recalled the diamond bezel Longines watch that Julius "Lovin' Putty" Annixter, one of the Outfit's gambling kingpins, had given Barney after the Canzoneri fight, and then his brow creased as he remembered how the watch had ended up: pawned off for peanuts or in the hands of some so-called friend when Barney was down on his luck. "He also had a beautiful platinum pinky ring with a three-and-three-quarter-carat diamond. In today's money it would be worth sixteen thousand dollars. He sold the ring for short money once he was an addict."

I asked him for his recollections of his father, Isidore, but there weren't many clear ones. George had been born in 1917, making him only six years old when his father was murdered in the holdup. He had vague memories of the funeral: his mother's howling in Yiddish; the coffin being carried down the stairs and into the hearse on Jefferson Street. "Pa was killed in December '23, and by early '24, I was in the Marks Nathan Jewish orphanage." To me, that orphan home conjured up images of a place as grim as Dickens's unnamed "public building" where motherless boys and foundlings go "without the inconvenience of too much food or clothing." But George's years there, he said, had hardly been so bleak.

"At the time, we thought it was terrible, but in retrospect, they were the best years of my life. I came out of it a musician. I came out with a wonderful Jewish education. And it wasn't until I came out that I got to know my older brothers. I'd missed a lot of years. We didn't get to visit an awful lot when I was in the orphan home. I came out finally in January of '33 and Barney won the title from Tony Canzoneri in June of '33."

He still fondly recalled almost all his brother's big bouts—except for the Henry Armstrong match, which "wasn't a fight," George said, "it was a tragedy. If Barney had been younger, if he could have had just one or two years back, he would have outmaneuvered Armstrong. But that's life; happens to all of us. For the first four and a half rounds he was handling Henry so easily. When the bell rang at the end of the fourth round, I could see that something was wrong, his legs were shot, he barely made it to the corner. From that point he was nothing but a punching bag." George said he'd wanted to walk out of the Madison Square Garden Bowl after the seventh round, but "my mother was sitting a few rows behind, and I didn't want her to see that I was giving up." Coming back to Chicago on the overnight train, "Barney's head was a watermelon. They had us in a bedroom car on the train, his barber was along, Harry the Barber—and by carefully applying the hot towels, by the time we got off the train in Chicago, with a pair of dark glasses on, Barn looked almost passable. God, it was rough seeing him like that. What bothered him so much was the fact that so many of the guys lost money on him. I said, 'C'mon, Barn, they rode the gravy train when you were hot.' "

George spoke like a character lifted from the pages of *The Adventures of Augie March* ("I am an American, Chicago-born—Chicago, that somber city—and go at things as I have taught myself, free-style, and will make the record in my own way: first to knock, first admitted; sometimes an innocent knock, sometimes a not so innocent . . ."). He shot me a wistful smile as he remembered how his brother Barney guided him through the awkward years of young adulthood: "When I was old enough, I didn't have to go down to Wabash Avenue and pay two dollars, Barney got some of the show-girls that he knew who taught me the business—taught me what life is supposed to be like."

I told him that I'd been reading about how so many of the boxers of Barney's era had gone into the Coast Guard—Jack Dempsey ran a boxing program and had a whole cadre dubbed "Dempsey Boys," including professionals like Lou Ambers, Marty Servo, Johnny Colan, Danny Kapilow, Lew Jenkins, who toured, fighting, for the entertainment of the troops. And other famous champions like Joe Louis, who enlisted in the Army in 1942, also spent much of their years in the service participating in boxing exhibitions. George nodded when I mentioned it. "Yeah, Barney was offered a commission in the Coast Guard," he said.

So why then had he insisted on enlisting in the Marines? Why had he asked to see combat?

George's response was initially cryptic: "Listen, he's my brother and I love him. But I can also see the things he did in his life—things that are nothing to talk about." I left it at that. We finished our Chinese food, broke open our fortune cookies. A little later in the night, after I'd driven to a Walgreen's so we could pick up a six-pack of Budweiser, George returned to his thought. "He'd gone through money like shit through a tin horn. He was down and he was disgusted. He'd gone up so high in his career, and when he came down, he came *way* down. I talked to him many, many times. There was no reasoning with him. At that point he felt there was no place left to go. He figured, what the hell, I'll go out fighting. He didn't plan for what happened. It was a freak occurrence. That night on Guadalcanal made a folk hero out of him. He came back smelling like a rose."

When we returned to George's apartment in Niles, he sat in his armchair watching the day's sports highlights on ESPN and I returned to sifting through the cache of vintage clippings and photographs; then he told me a story that had never been told before, about the depths of the suicidal depression Barney had sunk to by early 1942.

"He sent me letters when he went into the Marines, when he was stationed in California. He was saying good-bye to me. He didn't expect to come back alive. What he wrote in those letters . . ." George's voice trailed off and it took him a long moment to regain his composure before finishing the thought. "I start to break down when I think of it now. I tore them up, shredded them. So nobody would ever get a chance to see them."

Perhaps, I thought, thumbing through the stacks of yellowed newsprint and surviving family letters, in some strange way, little Yunk in the quiet isolation of his Marks Nathan Orphan Home had become a more fully rounded Jew than his famous older brother, Beryl, who with the Samson-like heroism of his boxing career, had come to embody the underside, indeed the ultimate sadness, of a life defined by physical prowess.

4

When Barney Ross arrived in San Diego in the spring of 1942, the streets were splashed in the kind of sunlight he hadn't seen in years—it must have taken him back momentarily to his days fighting in L.A., just out of the Golden Gloves, still scrambling to make a name for himself fighting in Jackie Fields's shadow. He was thirty-three, "ancient" for a Marine private going through basic training; the other boots called him "Grandpa." The years of drinking and smoking heavily in the cocktail lounge had taken their toll. The once granitelike abdomen had turned doughy; there was a double chin, whiskers speckled with silver, threads of white in his jet-black hair. He was surrounded by eighteen- and nineteen-year-olds, straw-headed kids who'd been in elementary school when he'd been trading blows with Tony Canzoneri and Jimmy McLarnin in the Chicago Stadium and the Polo Grounds. By July his instructors had him in a pith helmet, running him through the bayonet course. In the newspapers there appeared a photograph of Private Barney Ross, "ex-lightweight and two-times [*sic*] welterweight champion of the world . . . practic[ing] the upward jab with the 'long knife.' The former champ is waiting to finish 'boot camp' so he can enter the ring for the 'big battle.' " He earned his sharpshooter's medal and was

Private Barney Ross, USMC, in boot camp.

named "Honor Man," or the best platoon recruit among his class in San Diego.

On the last day of basic training, Cathy Howlett came out to San Diego so that Barney could marry her in a quiet civil ceremony—a far cry from the Orthodox ceremony to Pearl at the Congress Hotel in 1937, with the hordes of press and autograph hunters parked outside—attended only by Cathy's daughter, Noreen, and a handful of Barney's new Marine buddies. It took Sarah Rasofsky a long time to come to terms with the idea of intermarriage. Eventually though, Cathy won her over. She learned a smattering of Yiddish, and always marked the *yahrzeit* of Barney's father on the calendar and reminded him to light a candle. Eventually, when the other mothers on Roosevelt Road made cutting remarks about Barney marrying a *shikseh*, a fast-living showgirl, George Rasof recalls his mother telling them in Yiddish, "What should I do? Stop loving my son?"

His commanding officer felt he would be valuable to the war effort stationed in Camp Pendleton, teaching new boots hand-to-hand self-defense. Ross argued that he'd boxed almost all his adult life and hadn't enlisted in the Corps to spend the war throwing jabs and hooks in the hot Southern California sun, but he accepted the temporary assignment teaching mass boxing to fifteen platoons at a time. After six weeks he asked again to be transferred and was shipped out with the next troopship heading overseas, leaving as part of the Fleet Marine Force.

He set sail in late August, landing at Pago Pago in American Samoa. He spent six weeks on that "bare and grubby" island, training for the jungle fighting and amphibious landings that were to come. On Pago Pago we have another of those moments that read like fables, the sort of bare-knuckle legends that swirled around Daniel Mendoza or Dutch Sam in London's East End. In light of the hellish combat to come on Guadalcanal, the story almost feels like a comic prelude in a Shakespearean tragedy. The last prizefight of Barney Ross's career must have occurred sometime in September 1942, though reports of it didn't arrive on American shores until months later.

Barney Ross

United Press International

Barney Ross, ex-welterweight champ now doing his fighting with the Marines in the Southwest Pacific, recently knocked out a 215-pound Samoan boxing idol and in return was offered a native chieftain's daughter in marriage and a chance to share the tribe's crown with the chief.

The feat was revealed in letters here from Ben Malamude, a former Pittsburgh basketball player, now a pharmacist second-class in the Navy. Malamude said that Ross reluctantly agreed to take on the Samoan, who "was giving our Army and Navy heavyweights a going-over." The prestige of the Marines was at stake, and the match was finally made.

Ross recounted for a United Press reporter, stationed with the troops in the South Pacific, how a contingent of Marines had cleared a bivouac so he could fight the local heavyweight, a bare-chested strongman who insisted on having a few healthy shots of whiskey before brawling; and a crowd of hundreds of Marines and Samoan men had assembled, the ground scattered with cash-filled cigar boxes. His opponent was "one tough, hard, mean cookie. [He] wants to fight barefisted, which is alright with me, but Lieutenant Murdock wouldn't hold still for it, so we put on 16-ounce gloves and had a three-round tussle. We fought under Marquis of Queensberry rules, but this baby didn't mess around and I was sort of out of practice. Nevertheless, science did the trick and he went to sleep on the deck." Ross said he had declined the offer of the chief's daughter in marriage. He also declined to share the chief's tribal crown.

5

By the end of October 1942, Ross put aboard the SS *Matsonia*, a luxury liner of the Matson Lines that had been requisitioned as a troopship. He was now a member of the 2nd Marine Division, jocularly known as "the Howling Marines" in reference to the division's commander, General Holland "Howling Mad" Smith. The 2nd Marines were ordered into full battle dress and had little doubt about where they were headed. For weeks they'd been reading the articles in *Stars and Stripes* about how badly outnumbered and overwhelmed the 1st Marines were, trying to wrest from the Imperial Japanese Forces a fighter airstrip on Lunga Point (renamed Henderson Field) carved into a ninety-mile-long densely forested flank of the Mount Auster Volcano in the eastern Solomon Islands.

He couldn't know it at the time, of course, but Ross was about to be thrust into the epicenter of a campaign that later historians would call the turning point in the Pacific War. "For the Marines Guadalcanal was remembered as an epic struggle," historian John Keegan writes in *The Second*

World War. "Men who had fought there bore an aura of endurance which veterans of almost no other Pacific campaign acquired."

When the United States Marine Corps made its amphibious landing on Guadalcanal August 7, 1942, it marked the first land offensive by the United States against any Axis power. The Marines faced a ferocious Japanese counterattack, and the ensuing conflict evolved into a six-month struggle on land, in the air, and at sea. After many months of reading only about Allied forces being defeated and captured

Guadalcanal: Corporal Barney Ross of the United States Marine Corps with Father Fred Gehring, Catholic chaplain on Guadalcanal, as two "peace" birds alight on their shoulders on the "Island of Kill or Be Killed." (© *Bettmann*/CORBIS)

in the Philippines, on Wake Island and Guam, the American public looked anxiously for a victory in the South Pacific campaign.

In a quieter time that volcanic island might almost have held a dark magic: home to the world's largest freshwater crocodiles, several hundred species of orchids, butterflies as broad as a man's palm, and parrots with plumage in every shade from emerald-green to pomegranate-red. Those half-tame parrots lighted on the prizefighter's shoulders—we have the surviving photographs—and Ross and his fellow Marines looked at them as their mascots, calling them their "peace" birds.

But there was no peace to be found when Private Barney Ross waded onto the cleared beachhead of Guadalcanal on November 4, 1942, a member of B Company, 2nd Battalion, 8th Regiment, 2nd Marine Division. Japanese shells were exploding all around them. The Marines from the 1st Division were "walking corpses . . . covered in jungle mud." On his belly, Ross crawled to the forward foxholes, replacing the men from the 1st Division who collapsed like living skeletons. The forest was a cesspool of jungle rot, crawling bugs, leeches, and malarial mosquitoes. They were warned to watch for Japanese who crept "like ghosts" through the darkness. That first night on the Canal, the men in Barney's platoon lay in their foxholes with strings tied around their fingers to keep each other alert.

During the days, "the jungle sun fried us alive and the humidity was so bad I felt like I was back in the Turkish bath." The heavy tropical rains came without warning; then the tropical wasps and malarial mosquitoes, scorpions crawling inside pant legs. He did not remove his shoes and socks for two weeks.

6

On November 13, he watched the Naval Battle of Guadalcanal—first the sinking of two American cruisers, then the Japanese lost the *Hiei*, Japan's first downed battleship of the war. Overhead, Marine Grummans engaged in furious dogfights with Japanese Zeros. The planes strafed so low that one Marine shot a Zero down with his Reising submachine gun. Barney kept a tiny scrap of that Zero in his pocket throughout the war.

To accompany their sea assault, the Japanese launched a land attack to retake the island. American artillery bombarded the Japanese encampments. "They poured out of their positions screaming," Barney recalled. "But we stopped them with mortars, machine guns and grenades, and their dead piled up like so many hunks of meat in a butcher store. We held them off for four days, then our company got orders to move up." Ross and his platoon were among the Marines pushing forward past the Matanikau River. It was on this "dreadful night of November 19, 1942," as Barney later wrote in an *Esquire* magazine article, that he learned "fighting wasn't a game."

Captain Osborne K. ("O.K.") Le Blanc asked for volunteers to form a small patrol and scout ahead for the Army regiment that was advancing to take over from the Marines. Barney Ross stepped forward. On the afternoon of November 18, he and his patrol ran into a Japanese machine-gun nest, which they were able to knock out with mortars; seeing no other Japanese, they began to return to their company. But without warning they ran into a much larger party of Japanese who began firing machine guns. One young Marine from New Jersey, nicknamed "Whitey," was shot through the chest. Barney and another corpsman, the former professional golfer Dick "Heavy" Atkins, crawled on their bellies, pulling Whitey to cover. Atkins, Ross, and two other Marines named Monak and Freeman fashioned a makeshift stretcher from their coats and attempted to carry Whitey back down the Matanikau River. While the other Marines bore the weight of the stretcher, Barney faced the rear with his Browning Automatic Rifle. They had moved only several yards when more intense bursts of Japanese machine-gun fire strafed their party. Whitey was killed. Atkins, Monak, and Freeman were wounded.

Freeman and Atkins rolled into a depression in the jungle floor, Barney leapt into a freshly created shell crater, pulling Monak to safety with him. Monak, Freeman, and Atkins were too weak to handle their guns, so Barney took his Browning Automatic Rifle and fired off the eighty rounds he had remaining, then he took the other Marines' Brownings and, twisting and rolling, firing from ever-shifting positions, he tried to give the enemy the illusion of a stronger force.

In the midst of the gun battle, two infantrymen who had become detached from their regiment crawled into the shell crater alongside Barney Ross. They were also too badly wounded to fight. Barney took their Garand rifles, and as the infantrymen loaded, Barney continued to fire. His palms were soon "burning from the hot barrels of the six guns." The Marine Corps later calculated that Ross had fired over 350 rounds of ammunition. Out of bullets, he now began to heave hand grenades in the direction of the Japanese positions. Darkness fell in the jungle; the artillery shells kept exploding in the swampy green soil. The Japanese gunfire inched closer, and a fallen tree was, Barney later wrote, "a godsend . . . bullets kept bouncing off it. My helmet was a godsend, too. At least twenty bullets richoted off the log and my tin hat, bouncing off again."

He calculated the range of a Japanese machine-gunner. He didn't dare rise, so, lying flat on his belly, he lobbed three grenades in fast succession. The machine-gun fire halted. He crawled over to the trench in which Heavy Atkins and Freeman lay bleeding. He unhooked the grenades from their belts. As he crawled forward again, a mortar shell burst and shrapnel tore into his side, arm, and leg. In the darkness, he did his best to dress his own shrapnel wounds.

The low-hanging leaves began to patter with a hard rain. He gathered the rainwater and did his best to give Monak, Atkins, and Freeman a few drops to drink. The Japanese infantrymen were setting up at closer range, no more than thirty yards away. One of the infantrymen was struck again. A slug tore through Barney's left ankle and, screaming, he had to cut his boot away with his knife.

The pain was so intense that he felt himself losing consciousness. Delirious, feverish, shaking—he didn't yet realize he was suffering from the malaria that would plague him for years to come—he was convinced that if he blacked out he'd never awaken. He had twenty-two grenades—in some versions of the firefight it is twenty-one—and threw all except one, which he planned to hold in reserve should the Japanese soldiers storm into the foxhole, ready to die like Eliezar, baring his blade under the lead war elephant in I Maccabees.

Barney lay in the foxhole for some thirteen hours—a cruel "lifetime," he would later call it—watching over the wounded Marines and infantrymen. "I never expected to get out. I was crying, and praying, and shooting, and throwing grenades, and half the time, I guess, I was out of my head." Throughout the night he had comforted himself by repeating the Sh'ma Yisroel—"Hear O Israel, the Lord is God, the Lord is One." He prayed for himself, the wounded Marines and infantrymen, and "anybody else who was ready to die." In his delirium he saw the visage of a living dead man, bearded, in soiled apron, surrounded by paper sacks in the nameless grocery on Jefferson Street. "You have no idea how I talked to Pa throughout that night," Barney later told his brother George.

7

By the time reinforcements arrived, Freeman had bled to death. Barney was barely able to stand, but he helped to save the lives of Atkins and Monak, who would both require leg amputations. Atkins weighed 215 pounds to Ross's 140, but he somehow found the strength to drag the private to safety: "By half-crawling and half-walking we reached the main lines. Bullets were still coming a mile a minute. Every seven or eight yards we fell flat on our faces." Around that shell crater, Captain Le Blanc and Lieutenant Murdock surveyed the carnage, and it was later calculated that Ross had single-handedly killed twenty-two Japanese soldiers and saved untold American lives by halting the patrol's stealth advance. Informed that he was being recommended for distinguished service honors, Ross remarked to the United Press reporter stationed with the Marines in Guadalcanal, "Tell 'em to give it to my company. This is no one-man show." His body torn by shrapnel and bullets, feverish with malaria, he was evacuated to an aid station, where he was given quinine and atabrine. While he was in his fever, one of the aid men brought him a strange form of tribute—a "voodoo cane" made by a Solomon Islander, dark polished wood inset with six human teeth taken from a slain Japanese soldier. Barney would carry it throughout the rest of his stay in Guadalcanal, and on subsequent tours of the United States—as he addressed thousands at war-bond rallies and in munitions factories across the United States—he wielded the cane as if it were the rod of Moses.

As he was convalescing on the Canal, he was promoted to the rank of corporal. He was later awarded the Silver Star medal "for conspicuous gallantry and intrepidity in action against the enemy while serving with a Marine battalion on

Guadalcanal November 18–20, 1942." When the United Press reporter first wrote up his long night in the foxhole, on December 4, he downplayed his personal heroics. "As he told this correspondent today, 'the ring is kid's play compared to the battle out here—this is a finish fight with no holds barred and no referee to break the clinches.' "

He recovered enough to be sent back to the frontline action five more times, as the Marines and Army units continued to drive the retreating Imperial Japanese Forces northward through the jungle. In a matter of a few weeks—we should discount Barney's rhetorical use of "overnight" in various accounts—his hair had gone iron-gray with thick shocks of white. There is an eerie echo of the pogrom in Brest-Litovsk, when his father's hair had gone white, although of course Barney in Guadalcanal was an armed American Marine, while his father was a powerless Eastern European Jew.

It was in an aid tent on Lunga Point that he met the man who would become his most steadfast friend through the horrendous times to come. Father Frederic P. Gehring, the Navy chaplain assigned to the 1st Marine Division, had stormed the beach in the initial August 7 landing. Known as the "Padre of Guadalcanal," Gehring had accrued his own wartime legend in the Solomon campaign with the rescue of a six-year-old Chinese girl, Patsy Li, about whom he later wrote a book called *Child of Miracles*. She had been brought to Gehring's tent, having survived being "bayonetted by Japanese soldiers and left for dead in a Guadalcanal ditch, her body wracked with malaria and the impression of a rifle butt imprinted on her smashed skull." Gehring nursed her back to health, and their story was brought to national attention in a series of articles by *New York Times* war correspondent Foster Hailey. Gehring would later became the first naval chaplain to be awarded the Legion of Merit.

Barney Ross had heard the stories of Father Gehring ministering last rites to dying Marines, and he wandered into the priest's tent late in 1942, wanting nothing more than company. The priest watched as this once-elite athlete, his face now gaunt and sallow, began to shake violently, wrapping himself in blankets from the malarial chills but declining medical attention. The Brooklyn-born Gehring was an avid boxing fan, and he told Barney that he had followed all his big fights in New York, even though, as a good Catholic, he had been steadfastly rooting for Jimmy McLarnin. A photograph survives of the former prizefighter and the Vincentian priest in boxing gloves and sweat-soaked fatigues, putting on an impromptu sparring exhibition on the beach of Guadalcanal.

Around his neck, Barney still wore the small silver mezuzah he'd begun to wear before the first McLarnin fight; now he coupled it with the saint's medal Father Gehring gave him to help him through the "darkest night" of Guadalcanal. "Orthodox Jewish faith was the rock that sustained him and enabled him to overcome calamities that would have crushed other men," Gehring wrote years later in a *Reader's Digest* portrait of Barney entitled "The Most Unforgettable Character I Ever Met." He observed that

Ross was well versed in all the major religions and was practicing "ecumenicism" long before the word gained popular currency. There was no Jewish chaplain on Guadalcanal, but Father Gehring, who had learned to read Hebrew, and Barney Ross arranged for regular Shabbat services.

"The Christmas Eve of 1942 was a night nobody who was on the Canal will ever forget," Ross remembered later. Several hundred men of all faiths knelt in the mud outside a tent containing a makeshift altar; the regular chapel had been destroyed by Japanese artillery. "In the darkness we could hear the crackle of gunfire as the Japanese tried to infiltrate the Marine perimeter," Gehring recalled. After conducting the Mass in Latin, he asked for the gathering of Marines, sailors, and infantrymen to join him in some carols. Gehring was a trained violinist, but there was no one in the gathering who knew how to manage the pump organ that had been brought from the nearby island of Tulagi expressly for the services. The *New York Times* later described the scene:

> Finding someone to play his little pump organ might not have been a miracle, but some sort of chuckling divine intervention does seem to be the most logical explanation for the fact that the only man on Guadalcanal who knew how to play the organ was Barney Ross, a decorated war hero, who surely could not have just happened to be Jewish. Painstakingly learning the carols note by note, Ross obligingly pumped out "Silent Night" and the rest of the Christian canon.

With the end of the Midnight Mass, Father Gehring asked Barney to speak. Ross said that, it being Christmastime, a lot of the men on the Canal were missing their mothers. "I've been thinking about my mother, too, and I've got a favorite song I'd like to play and sing in her honor." He didn't have to glance at the keys; those chords were as familiar as the *BR* tattooed on his forearm. His personal fighting theme; a song first made famous by Sophie Tucker, with lyrics by Jack Yellen and melody by Lew Pollack. In the *Reader's Digest*, Father Gehring recalled many of those leathernecks, sailors, and infantrymen—malnourished and unshaven, some recent amputees, boys who knew that they would likely never return to their mothers—were openly weeping as Barney Ross sang "My Yiddishe Momme."

8

In February 1943, more Japanese destroyers were sighted approaching Guadalcanal. The Marines initially feared this was another reinforcement action, similar to the one of the past November. But the Japanese were abandoning their positions in the Solomons. During the next few days, in near secrecy, the Japanese evacuated more than 11,000 men, while the American forces engaged in sporadic battles against the few ships that they spotted. On February 9, when troops from the 132nd Infantry and the 161st Infantry met in a village on the Tenamba River, having spotted nothing but empty Japanese camps and discarded material, General

Alexander P. Patch, commander of all U.S. ground troops on the island, radioed Vice Admiral William "Bull" Halsey: "Total and complete defeat of Japanese forces on Guadalcanal effected 1625 today. The Tokyo Express no longer has terminus on Guadalcanal."

Of the 60,000 deployed Army and Marine Corps troops, 1,592 were killed in action. Navy losses (including Marine aviators) were 5,041. Japanese casualties were much higher, more than 20,000, fully two-thirds of all Japanese forces stationed on Guadalcanal. The six-month Battle of Guadalcanal was a devastating blow to the morale of the Imperial Japanese Forces and, coupled with the February 2 surrender of the German 6th Army at Stalingrad, sent the signal that the tide of war might finally be turning in the Allies' favor. "Before Guadalcanal the enemy advanced at his pleasure," Bull Halsey later said. "After Guadalcanal he retreated at ours."

By early February, Barney Ross had suffered a severe malarial attack and had been evacuated to a field hospital on the island of Efate in the New Hebrides. He convalesced for twelve days, drifting in and out of consciousness, racked by hallucinations, chills, and dysentery. He had lost thirty pounds since the night in the shell crater. Shell-shocked, he screamed in hysteria and had to be restrained. He had debilitating migraines. The shrapnel and bullet fragments brought a kind of chronic pain that never fully left him; decades later, his brother George recalled, if a bedsheet so much as brushed across Barney's left ankle, he would wince again at the shooting pain.

The corpsmen tried to ease his pain by administering half-grain syrettes of morphine. For a time he thought he'd found the "keys of paradise" that Thomas De Quincey had described in 1822, the rapture of "just, subtle and mighty Opium." He wrote later, "The morphine lifted me out of the snake pit and let me climb high in the clouds." In that floating instant the pain subsided, the malarial convulsions eased. Though he was instructed to use morphine in moments of extreme pain, some of the medics began to offer him extra shots. When he was transferred from Efate to a base hospital in Auckland, New Zealand, the supply of morphine was steadier. He had his own stash of syrettes and learned to inject himself. It marked the beginning of an inexorable descent he was able to keep hidden from the world for more than three years.

PART SIX

1

Barney arrived back in San Diego on February 26, 1943, onboard the SS *Matsonia*, the same converted luxury liner that had first ferried him to American Samoa; onboard he was already experiencing another attack of malaria, made worse by the cravings for morphine. He limped ashore with the aid of his "voodoo cane" and, as *The New York Times* reported, "kneeled humbly . . . and kissed the ground today. . . . 'This I vowed to do, if ever I saw American soil again—sometimes out there we're not so sure we shall.' " By early March 1943, his beaming, gap-toothed smile was once again on the front pages of newspapers across the nation. He was at a new apex of his fame, the accolades for Corporal Barney Ross (USMC) eclipsing even the glow of his lightweight and welterweight championship glory. His face would soon appear on Ringside bubblegum cards; he even had a Barney Ross candy bar.

His action in the Solomons had been widely reported while he was still recovering in the hospitals on Efate and in Auckland. On February 17, 1943, the New York Boxing Writers' Association named Ross the winner of the Edward J. Neil Memorial Award as the sport's "Man of the Year." The prize was a posthumous tribute to Neil, the Associated Press correspondent killed by a bomb at the age of thirty-seven while covering the Spanish Civil War. At the sold-out gala— some 1,500 of the requests for tickets had to be denied by organizers—former New York mayor Jimmy Walker spoke, as did Barney's friends, Lieutenant Commander Jack Dempsey, Commander Gene Tunney, and Lieutenant James J. Braddock, the former heavyweight champion, later mythologized by Hollywood as "The Cinderella Man." A naval officer accepted the award on behalf of the wounded former champion.

On March 6, Hearst's *Chicago Herald-American* announced a scoop, the first serialization of "Barney Ross's Own Story of Guadalcanal." He was depicted on the cover of the March issue of Nat Fleischer's *The Ring*, improbably attired in full Marine battle dress and helmet, wearing a pair of ox-blood-colored boxing gloves. He penned—or more likely dictated, since it's hard to imagine the impatient Barney playing with a page of prose—an *Esquire* magazine story of the fighting on November 18–20, describing the dead Marines scattered around him, and the ones clinging to life, in the kind of unabashed propaganda that filled glossy American magazines in the era: "What was I fighting for?" he wrote. "I was fighting for my life and for America, and my buddies, and for home . . . and for the things we believed in. I was fighting for our kind of world."

He was granted a few days' sick leave; he went to Hollywood to reunite with his wife, Cathy—she'd been dancing in clubs and landed a few minor film roles—made the scene in his Marine dress uniform, mingling with movie stars in Hollywood nightclubs, and was asked by Eddie Cantor, the former *Ziegfeld Follies* headliner, to give an address to the nation during his popular radio broadcast. His family back on Roosevelt Road were photographed in the Chicago papers gathered in the living room as they listened to Barney's voice live from San Diego.

His Hollywood talent agent, Lou Irwin, had, shortly after Barney's arrival in the States, begun fielding calls from studio heads and the "top screen stars" looking to play the role of the prizefighter-turned-Marine in a film adaptation: John Garfield, Jimmy Cagney, and George Raft all were vying for the chance to portray Barney Ross in a feature film.

The War Department too recognized his value to the nation's morale. Ross was scheduled for a mid-March Red Cross rally in New York with Eleanor Roosevelt. On the way east, arrangements were made for a one-day stopover in Chicago. CITY GREETS HERO BARNEY ROSS: RECORD OVATION MEETS CHICAGO'S FIGHTING MARINE, read the banner headline in the March 11 *Chicago Daily News* to a story surrounded by the news that the British were pounding Rommel heavily in North Africa, that members of the French underground had killed at least 250 Nazis in an act of sabotage on a troop train, and, this being Chicago after all, a report that a still-unnamed West Side loan shark, the "Financial Genius of the Capone Mob," was being "quizzed by a federal grand jury" about the Mob's labor activities in the 24th Ward.

"Corp. Barney Ross, dubbed a 'good marine' by his commander on Guadalcanal, came back to the old hometown today and got the greatest ovation in his career as a fighting man." He was greeted by Mayor Ed Kelly and a horde of reporters at Municipal Airport, dressed in his dark field uniform, khaki shirt, dark tie, and Marine cap. "Ross's hair isn't streaked with gray as when he left. It's snow white. He smiles through a tropic-tanned complexion, but it isn't a youthful smile. Barney Ross looks very tired, weary." His mother in a black mink coat and lace-trimmed black hat plants a kiss on Beryl's sunburned cheeks; his brothers in fedoras surround him as he addresses the crowd. Together they rode in an open car down Michigan Avenue to the Treasury Center in the Loop. This was not the "riotous welcome" he had heard in the ticker-tape parades after beating Canzoneri and McLarnin but a "war-serious crowd hail[ing] its returning son . . . its comparative silence a tribute," the *Daily News* reported, "not to jaw busting [but] for Jap busting." Ross stayed in Chicago only six hours—enjoying his mother's dish of "fried matzohs"—before flying on to New York, where a full agenda of speeches awaited.

The relentless pace was too much for a man just discharged from the hospital in San Diego, now jet-lagged and still battling lingering effects of shrapnel wounds, shell shock, and malaria. On March 13, he was honored by a sellout crowd at Madison Square Garden, formally accepting the Edward J. Neil Memorial Trophy from former mayor Jimmy Walker, to the accompaniment, as *The New York Times* reported, of "as sincere and moving an outburst of cheering as has ever been heard there."

It was a tense moment when Ross marched the short distance from the runway to the ring, preceded by three Red Cross nurses, the American flag and a Red Cross banner. Ross, gray-haired now despite his youth, stood visibly shaken and sobbing while Colby M. Chester, general chairman of the New York Red Cross Committee, made a brief speech extolling the champion. Ross then spoke, hesitantly at first but later more confidently, in praise of all the members of our fighting forces everywhere and in praise of the Red Cross. [Former Mayor] Walker pointed out that the "neighbors were happy because Barney Ross came home. Remember, we know that you were born in New York."

Ross fell ill immediately after the award ceremony but recovered well enough that by March 15, accompanied by his wife, Cathy, he could address a small Red Cross gathering in the lobby of the New York Life Insurance Building. Then, as he was preparing to depart for a climactic Red Cross war fund rally in Madison Square Garden, he collapsed unconscious in his suite in the Astor Hotel. Cathy called an ambulance, and he was rushed to the U.S. Naval Hospital in St. Albans, Queens. He had a 104-degree fever and the malaria was full-blown again. Barney insisted that Cathy take his place on the stage at the rally, where she read a prepared address before the 20,000 in Madison Square Garden; in her hand she clutched the wooden cane inset with Japanese teeth. "This is the first time Barney hasn't answered the bell," she said, then collapsed herself. Mrs. Roosevelt held her, and the First Lady assured the crowd that Barney Ross was expected to make a full recovery.

Recuperating in his St. Albans hospital bed, he was formally awarded the Silver Star medallion, received sergeant's chevrons, and was informed that he would be receiving the Presidential Unit Citation. He was also transferred from active duty in the 2nd Battalion, 8th Marine Regiment, to the Naval Industrial Incentive Division, with responsibility to tour the country addressing Red Cross rallies and war plants and to use his personal narrative of survival and sacrifice as a morale-boost for civilian factory workers and war-weary wives.

The doctors at St. Albans advised him that he was too

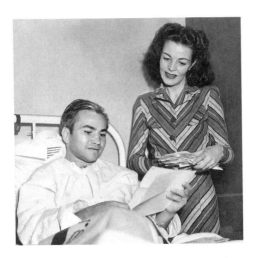

Corporal Ross is visited by his wife, Cathy,
at St. Albans Naval Hospital, Queens,
New York, March 17, 1943.

run-down, that he should spend a month recovering. Cathy put her dancing and acting career on hold to travel the country with Barney. After one month in the naval hospital in Queens, he commenced a seemingly nonstop tour that would last through much of 1943 and much of 1944, making hundreds of personal appearances and radio addresses. On one 1943 weekend trip he spoke at the Eversharp Pencil Corporation, the Rockola jukebox plant, made a radio broadcast on Milwaukee's WTMJ, then an appearance at the Buda Company of Harvey, Illinois—then held an "open house" in suites at the Morrison Hotel, where one of the guests told a reporter, "He'll probably ask for reshipment to Guadalcanal to get a rest."

2

In late November, he traveled to the White House with his mother for a Rose Garden ceremony at which he received a presidential citation from President Roosevelt for his "great personal courage and sincere devotion to his comrades." And there was news from Hollywood: Lou Irwin had now struck a deal with John Garfield to produce a feature film of *The Barney Ross Story*. Garfield, born Julius Garfinkle, the son of an immigrant Jewish tailor on the Lower East Side, had recently left his contract at Warner Brothers to start his own company, Enterprise Studios, with the aim of shooting independent films with "political relevance." Garfield would become, in the estimation of film historian Gerald Mast, "perhaps the prototypical *film noir* hero." Garfield and his partner, Bob Roberts, hired screenwriter Arnold Manoff (like Garfield, he would later be blacklisted) to begin work on a script about the rough-edged Maxwell Street boy who watches his father's murder, then rises phoenixlike to world's champion boxer and hero of Guadalcanal.

Ross meanwhile was touring the country addressing warbond and blood-bank rallies; he began to suffer relapses—shakes and chills and high fevers. Cathy would bury him under wool blankets and give him quinine, but nothing seemed to help. He remembered the reverie of his morphine syrettes; he began to crave the illusion of euphoria and began to visit private doctors, complaining of migraines and chronic pain from shrapnel wounds. Few doctors could refuse a Silver Star hero of the Battle of Guadalcanal. But each morphine injection seemed to wear off more quickly than the last, and it got to the point that when he arrived in a city he would look up one doctor in the morning and a second before catching a train or flight out of town. When doctors would no longer supply him, he went to street connections to get his hands on pilfered military morphine. He was still trying to closely guard the desperate secret; he would tell Cathy that he had to visit a Guadalcanal Marine buddy, then sneak off to try to score. He learned all the addict tricks, that in the paregoric medicine sold over the counter, there was a small amount of opiate. He could drink the paregoric straight and get a mild high, or he could boil the paregoric down until a tiny amount of the narcotic was in the bottom of the pot, which could then be injected with a hypodermic needle.

He received his honorable discharge from the United States Marine Corps on April 11, 1944. He was granted a medical disability; his height was listed as "66-1/2 inches," his complexion as "ruddy," and his character "excellent." Cathy had settled in Hollywood, with her daughter, Noreen, the only child from her first marriage. She was dancing in small movie roles now, largely forgettable productions like the wartime musical *Bamboo Blonde*. Visiting friends who saw the seemingly glamorous couple in their California home were taken aback by how bad Barney looked. "It was obvious that he was not well," wrote Father Gehring, "but I didn't know enough about the symptoms of drug addiction to realize that his war ailments had been compounded by something more sinister." The former fighter no longer had muscle tone; his face was puffy and hollow-eyed. "He was so ashamed of his addiction that he couldn't bear to tell anyone about it."

One night just after the war's end, his brother George received a call at H. Horowitz & Company, a jewelry store in the Loop. "Barn was staying at a hotel maybe two blocks away. He says, 'Yunk, whattaya doin' tonight? Can you stop by?' He needed to borrow some money, I lent it to him. He was lying in bed and shaking. Suffering with malaria. Couldn't keep warm. He says, 'Get a hold of housekeeping.' I went to the telephone, but he says, 'No, that'll take too long. Go downstairs, get me some more blankets.' I couldn't see it at the time. But he wanted me out of the way. He had the shakes from it. He needed his fix."

3

He had "learned the junk equation," as William Burroughs called it in his 1952 novel *Junkie*. Burroughs had also developed a habit through morphine syrettes in the mid-1940s. "Junk is not, like alcohol or weed, a means to increased enjoyment of life. Junk is not a kick. It is a way of life."

Ross, "muddled and despondent," kept pressing Lou Irwin to get more advances from John Garfield for the film version of his life story. The entire advance for the film, he later said, had been injected into his arms. He was frequenting known drug-dealing locations like Sixth and Main in Hollywood, wearing sunglasses in the night so no one would recognize that this celebrated war hero had become a fiend. "I spent $250,000 on drugs in four years," he later estimated. "Some of it was for buying silence. I paid through the nose." Most of that money wasn't even his; he borrowed from family, friends, and from loan sharks; at one point he even went to Jewish gangsters like Abner "Longy" Zwillman, the notorious Newark mob boss, who had always been a big fan and bet heavily on Barney's fights. He took sporadic jobs refereeing fights but was sliding into a financial abyss.

He finally called up Milton Blackstone, the public-relations executive who had first brought him to train at

Grossinger's resort back in 1934, begging for a job. Blackstone, who was now managing the career of the teenage crooner named Eddie Fisher, had told Ross that he could always come to work for the Blackstone Advertising Agency.

He flew to New York and took the first desk job in his life on West 57th Street, officially handling client relations—making public appearances. Blackstone and his brother also owned the Eureka Shipbuilding Company in Newburgh, New York, and Barney's name was listed on the books in the vague capacity of "recreation director." He wasn't much of an employee. He lived in the Edison Hotel and kept his needles and heroin locked in a drawer. He could never put in a full day in the office; he would find himself nodding, drifting, glassy-eyed. He'd sneak out to Broadway movie theaters and would ride the subways for hours. He nodded off once on a train to Philadelphia and was pickpocketed. At a gala Manhattan dinner in 1946, as he was being honored for charitable work he'd done in the garment industry, he could barely mumble his thanks on the dais and nearly collapsed with symptoms of heroin withdrawal.

In late 1946 he saw a copy of one of the New York papers and read that "Cathy Ross has been granted a provisional divorce." He realized that he had only one option left to him: commitment to the "federal narcotics farm" at Lexington, Kentucky, which was widely known among junkies as the place to go for a so-called "reduction cure" and detoxification. The Clinical Research Center of the U.S. Public Health Service Hospital in Lexington was opened in 1935 and began accepting neuropsychiatric patients in 1942. Ross combed his hair, washed his face, put on sunglasses to cover his reddened eyes, and took a taxi to the Federal Building in Lower Manhattan and asked for United States Attorney John F. X. McGohey, describing himself as a heroin addict and a war casualty.

"I started taking dope when I was in the hospital on Guadalcanal," Ross said, as quoted by Art Smith, a reporter for the *New York Evening Post*. "I had been sent there for shock and malaria and it was pretty tough. So a couple of buddies of mine, guys in my outfit, began giving me drugs. They meant only good and the dope helped me.

"The malaria kept coming back. Each time the drugs seemed to help. Finally I was discharged and I thought my troubles were over. But about a year later, the awful headaches came back again. Then the chills and the fever returned and I was up against the same old thing.

"I went back to the dope but, not being a doctor, I got in over my head this time. Now I've got to beat it the hard way. I want you to send me away until I'm all right again."

"It took a lot of courage to come up here, Barney," McGohey said.

"Not courage," Ross said. "Look at it this way: A lot of kids think I'm a hell of a . . . fighter. Well, I can't let 'em see me wind up as a dope fiend. I got to beat it."

McGohey placed Ross under arrest. There was no formal arraignment or bail hearing. The overcrowded conditions at Lexington made a criminal arrest the only way for Ross to be committed to the facility.

It made the evening papers—BARNEY ROSS, DOPE

ADDICT, GIVES UP—and there were news-flash bulletins on the radio: Ross, the former champion and Silver Star Marine sergeant had surrendered for arrest and commitment to Lexington. He drove up to the Catskills; Milton Blackstone had offered to fly him to Kentucky on the Grossinger's private plane. On board the plane he had his final fix—Blackstone watched as Barney Ross took out the heroin, eyedropper, and syringe and spiked his vein, then vowed it would be the last shot he'd ever give himself.

He flew into Cincinnati, then drove with Blackstone across the river and into the rolling bluegrass horse country, and entered the gates of the fortresslike complex of Lexington. He was sent to the withdrawal ward for the reduction method of Dr. Herbert Wieder. Burroughs, who turned himself into Lexington in 1948, describes in *Junkie* how the "method" worked:

> The cure at Lexington is not designed to keep the addicts comfortable. It starts at one-quarter of a grain of M three times a day and lasts eight days—the preparation now used is a synthetic morphine called dolophine. After eight days, you get a send-off shot and go over in "population." There you receive barbiturates for three nights and that is the end of medication. For a man with a heavy habit, this is a very rough schedule.

In his first day of withdrawal, Ross began to cramp and convulse. His legs kicked wildly, as if he were stricken by Saint Vitus's dance. He was supposed to continue on the reduced dosage of morphine for ten days, but on the fifth day he decided to go cold. His bed was surrounded by Hebrew prayer books, and he clutched at the mezuzah and Father Gehring's saint's medallion. In his delirium he saw Japanese soldiers spitting at him. He spat at his own reflection in the mirror. He saw "mountains caving in and I saw rivers washing over big cities and drowning them." Rattlesnakes hissed "streams of poison." This was a vision of hell, he thought, "a dark room with gray walls." He saw his father again in his apron at the Jefferson Street grocery, and as in that night in the shell crater in the Solomons, he called out, "Pa, Pa, ask God to have pity on your Beryl. . . ." He managed to break into a locker and took a shaving razor and attempted to cut his own throat; an older inmate jumped him and prevented the suicide attempt. "You've got a lot to live for," he said.

Barney's family in Chicago, imagining Lexington to be a kind of white-coat sanitarium, was shocked to see the harsh reality of his commitment to the Public Health Service Hospital. George Rasof and brother-in-law Irving "Lefty" Kaplan were the first to come visit, after Barney's sixth week. They flew into Cincinnati and took a cab across the river to Lexington. "They called it a public health hospital," George told me. "But, listen, it was a fuckin' jail. It was federal jail. When we got there, they took away our cigarettes, checked them thoroughly and gave them back to us. He came to see us across a big courtyard—drawn and gaunt. My brother-in-law Lefty was a rough-tough guy, strong as a mule, known for a violent temper. When he saw what had become of Barney, Lefty broke down in tears."

He didn't exercise the privilege of all voluntary patients to ask for release but remained until Dr. Victor Vogel decided that his addiction had been permanently "cured." His stay in Lexington lasted more than four months. Letters of support streamed in from so many of the men he'd battled in the ring: Tony Canzoneri, Jimmy McLarnin, Billy Petrolle, Ceferino Garcia, Henry Armstrong, who had become, in his retirement, an ordained Baptist minister. Regaining his vigor, he was put in charge of the gym and taught guards and Public Health Service officers jujitsu and boxing techniques. In long psychiatric sessions he "poured out his heart" about the murder of his father, his experiences on Guadalcanal, the times he'd contemplated killing himself.

Some skeptics claimed that Ross had been afforded a kind of celebrity red-carpet treatment and that Lexington officials were only too happy to exploit his release for public-relations purposes. (A headline carried by the United Press on January 12, 1947 read, ROSS CONQUERS NARCOTICS: ANOTHER K.O. FOR BARNEY.) Dr. Vogel, head medical officer in charge of the institution, announced that "Ross's victory over narcotics came sooner than expected," adding that the average period of time needed to cure an addict was about one year. Ross told the United Press that the fight against addiction was the toughest of his life. He was released on a sixty-day "furlough" and would voluntarily return to Lexington for further medical evaluation before declaring himself free from the grip of addiction. He sat with reporters over a breakfast of two eggs and toast, looking, at thirty-seven, like a man at least a decade older. Yet he was undeniably fit; his weight of 153 was only six pounds more than his fighting prime. He said he planned to return to Chicago to see his mother, brothers, and sister, and then was going to California to try to reconcile with his "showgirl wife." He credited the Jewish faith learned at his father's knee with helping him beat addiction, and when *Coronet* magazine ran a first-person account of his battle with addiction, it was titled "God Was in My Corner."

4

God might have been in his corner, but John Garfield no longer was. Ross often said that one of the lowest moments of his months in Lexington was reading in the papers that Garfield was no longer planning to make *The Barney Ross Story*. It was one thing to make a picture about a ghetto-reared prizefighter who becomes a war hero; but a tale of a full-blown heroin addict was still too taboo a topic for Hollywood. According to one account, screenwriter Arnold Manoff, hearing about Barney's commitment to Lexington, went to see his friend Abraham Polonsky on the Paramount lot. Polonsky and Manoff walked the two blocks to Enterprise Studios, and Polonsky composed the story of

Body and Soul, and within the afternoon found himself on loan from Paramount to write the script.

The outlines of Barney Ross's life were still openly discernible in *Body and Soul,* a morality tale set in the seedy world of boxing. The film was directed by Robert Rossen, grandson of a rabbi, who had grown up in poverty and surrounded by violence on the Lower East Side and had a brief career as a professional boxer. In the film, John Garfield plays a ghetto-reared prizefighter named Charley Davis—no overt references to Jewishness, of course—who makes a Faustian pact with racketeers. Polonsky and Rossen had scarcely tried to mask their debt to Barney's biography: there is the crucial scene in which the boxer's father (the proprietor of a New York candy store, not a Maxwell Street grocery) is murdered in his shop; but there are so many other familiar moments— the montage of Charley as champion, at the racetrack ripping up betting slips. Even in Polonsky's masterfully terse dialogue there are lines that sound to me as if they'd been dictated from Barney's mouth into the screenwriter's ear: "Here. Take the money, Ben. It's not like people. It's got no memory. It don't think." *Body and Soul* earned Garfield his only Academy Award nomination for Best Actor, 1947. The film won the Oscar for best editing and would be the only commercial and financial success Enterprise Pictures ever had. The cinematography, by James Wong Howe, was highly ingenious—cameras were for the first time mounted on roller skates to give the illusion of kinetic movement inside the ring. *Body and Soul,* considered a film noir classic, and *Raging Bull,* Martin Scorcese's 1980 rendering of Jake

La Motta's troubled life story, rank as the finest boxing movies ever made.

For Barney Ross, *Body and Soul* was like a sucker punch to the sternum. He engaged in a protracted lawsuit with John Garfield and Bob Roberts, and eventually settled for some $60,000, money that he said went to repaying advances his agent Lou Irwin had made during the years of his addiction. And when his story did find its way to the big screen, a decade later, the drug addiction that had so scared off Garfield had become the film's overarching theme. *Monkey on My Back*, directed by Hungarian-born André De Toth, was released in 1957, starring Cameron Mitchell as Ross. Scarcely watched today, the film is a well-meant if overly sincere melodrama, akin to the better-known *Man with the Golden Arm*, which starred Frank Sinatra in an adaptation of the Nelson Algren novel. The unsubtle marketing campaign embarrassed everyone in Barney's family. His brothers cringed when they saw the marquee for the world premier at Chicago's Woods Theater on Randolph Street, the giant blown-up picture of Cameron Mitchell spiking his arm, the bright streamers fluttering:

THE BARNEY ROSS STORY!

JUNKIE! IT MEANS DOPE-FIEND!

THE HOTTEST HELL ON EARTH!

Though he had been hired as a consultant to the production, Ross was disgusted with the final cut and publicly disowned the production: "Filth, bilge and cheap sensation." His mother could never bear to watch it.

Decades later, George Rasof told me he would immediately click away when *Monkey on My Back* aired on late-night television. For a man so deeply entrenched in Hollywood culture—who counted stars like Eddie Cantor, George Jessel, Jack Benny, and Eddie Fisher among his closest friends, and got personal horseracing tips from Louis B. Mayer—Ross felt singularly betrayed by the film industry. But there is something touchingly naive about Barney's expectation that the dreamworld of Hollywood—that glittering mirage invented by tough Jewish immigrants like himself—could rescue him from his present nightmare.

PART SEVEN

1

During much of the time of his narcotic addiction, Barney attended services regularly at the Actor's Temple on West 47th Street. The small synagogue, a vestige of the glory years of Jewish Broadway, boasted members like Sophie Tucker, Milton Berle, Florence Ziegfeld, and Al Jolson. In one recollection of his drug years, Barney tells us that he wandered into the *shul* to stand before the ark, praying for strength to fight the craving for heroin, but when Rabbi Bernard Birstein walked in, asking why he was so early for *mincha*, he fled the sanctuary in mute shame. When he was in Chicago, he went to the Anshei Lubavitch *shul* off Roosevelt Road with his family, still afforded the honor of getting called up first to the Torah.

But Barney's Jewish identification found larger expression than private worship.

There is a little-known, second narrative of his life, running parallel, like a set of ghostly tracks overgrown by wild grass, even in the grimmest years of his drug addiction. Holocaust scholar Rafael Medoff has written of Barney Ross as "one of the first professional athletes to use his stardom" in support of his political beliefs. At a time when many leading Jewish Americans remained silent, Ross was outspoken about the plight of Jews in Nazi-occupied Europe and used his celebrity to champion the creation of a Jewish state. In April 1943, Ross was a key participant in a Passover Seder broadcast over armed-service frequencies. While on his war-bond tour in Cleveland, making a radio address to 2,000 Navy men attending Pesach services at the U.S. Naval Training Station in Sampson, New York, Ross said that the Marines he had served with on Guadalcanal had a lot in common with the ancient Israelites crossing the Sinai: "They were on good terms with the Lord."

"For Our Kind of World," the first-person account of his Guadalcanal heroics, first published in *Esquire*, was anthologized by the National Jewish Welfare Board in a 1944 hardcover entitled *Fighting for America: An Account of Jewish Men in the Armed Forces, from Pearl Harbor to the Italian Campaign*. The aim of the book was to combat "eleventh-hour Nazi psychological warfare," the age-old stereotype of Jews as war profiteers, blackmarketeers, and draft-dodgers. ("This volume then is not only a book about the war, it is in a sense a weapon of war," reads the introduction, "a weapon with which to counteract enemy propaganda that seeks to cause division among Americans . . . that seeks to build up resentments, one for another, on a tissue of lies.")

But at least since the late 1930s, Ross and his closest circle of friends engaged in a more combative—and controversial— brand of activism, one that was more a product of the gangland legacy of Samuel "Nails" Morton than of Rabbi

Stephen Wise. There is considerable firsthand documentation for this period, owing largely to the November 1963 arrest of Jack Ruby in the murder of Lee Harvey Oswald. Ira Colitz, the son of a scrap-metal dealer, Barney's closest friend at the end of his life, and later an Illinois state senator, told FBI agents investigating Ruby's Chicago years how a group of Jewish friends who hung out in the Lawndale poolroom and in Davey Miller's restaurant on Kedzie and 12th Street were frequently in brawls involving homegrown Nazis:

> During the late 1930s there were many meetings in the Chicago area of the German-American Bund. These meetings were . . . generally against the Jewish people. Upon learning that a Bund meeting was being held, that information would be telephoned to places like the Lawndale Pool Hall, Dave Miller's Restaurant, and other hangouts of the Jewish following and they would automatically go to that meeting and attempt to break it up using violence. . . .

We don't know if Barney Ross was involved in any of these spontaneous anti-Nazi brawls—certainly his fame as a prizefighter would have made any arrest newsworthy—but it's quite probable that he was one of the leaders.

Then, during the later days of the Second World War, Barney Ross allied himself with the so-called Bergson Group, a small, intensely driven band of militant Zionists, disciples of the Revisionist leader Vladimir Jabotinsky, who were active in the United States as a front for the underground organization the Irgun Zvei Leumi, headed by Menachem Begin.

They gathered under a decidedly unwieldy banner, "The Committee for a Jewish Army of Stateless and Palestinian Jews," and were led by Peter Bergson, a pseudonym of the Lithuanian-born Hillel Kook—he had changed his name so as not to embarrass his family in the Yeshuv (pre-state Israel), where his uncle Yitzchak Kook was the chief rabbi— since both the British authorities and mainstream Zionist groups labeled the Irgun as "terrorists." Playwright and screenwriter Ben Hecht described the Irgun's political emissary as "a man in his thirties of medium height with a small blond mustache, an English accent, and a voice inclined to squeak under excitement." Hecht, who had been reading of the annihilation of European Jewry and "went through my days holding my anger like a hot stove in my arms," became a passionate advocate for the Bergson Group, and found himself denounced by Hollywood friends as a "fascist" and ostracized by mainstream Jewish organizations. According to Medoff: "For [Barney] Ross to support the controversial Emergency Committee took real political courage—the Committee's public criticism of the Allies' apathy toward the Holocaust had infuriated government officials in Washington and London. In fact, the State Department repeatedly tried to have the Emergency Committee's chairman, Peter Bergson, drafted or deported."

Just days after Ross's return to San Diego from the South

Pacific, the Bergson Group, through its newly formed Emergency Committee to Save the Jewish People of Europe, staged Hecht's impassioned "propaganda project," a pageant entitled *We Will Never Die*. Two sold-out performances were in Madison Square Garden on March 9, 1943, under a backdrop of "two towering tablets inscribed in Hebrew with the Ten Commandments." A rabbi opened a performance dedicated to the murdered Jews of Europe. "We are here to say our prayers for the two million who have been killed in Europe because they bear the names of your first children— the Jews. . . . We are not here to weep for them. We are here to honor them and to proclaim the victory of their dying. For in our Testament are written the words of Habakkuk, prophet of Israel, 'They shall never die.' "

In the subsequent weeks, *We Will Never Die* played Washington, Philadelphia, Boston, Chicago, St. Louis, and Los Angeles. According to Hecht, the "news and pictures of our pageant in the press were the first American newspaper reports on the Jewish massacre in Europe." The culmination of the Emergency Committee's activities was an all-star "Show of Shows" at Madison Square Garden on March 13, 1944, where a capacity crowd of 20,000 saw Bob Hope, Gracie Fields, Helen Hayes, Jimmy Durante, Ethel Merman, Zero Mostel, and Molly Picon. Milton Berle served as master of ceremonies, and musical numbers were performed by Paul Robeson, Perry Como, the Andrews Sisters, the Xavier Cugat band, and the Count Basie band. The next day's *New York Times* reported that "Sgt. Barney Ross, former boxing champion who fought at Guadalcanal, gave his mustering-out pay of $300 to buy 150 tickets for members of the armed forces as a means of aiding the committee."

2

Immediately after his discharge from the Public Health Service Hospital at Lexington, Ross continued to use his fame to drum up public support for what were then still known as "Palestinian" causes. In the spring of 1947, he headed up a committee sponsoring a goodwill tour of the United States by the Hapoel Haifa soccer team, kicking off with a match against American all-star players in Yankee Stadium on May 4. He also resumed his activities with the Bergson Group's American League for a Free Palestine, which sought to rally American support for the creation of a Jewish state. In January 1948, Irv Kupcinet's column reported that "Barney Ross, ex-champ and Marine hero, has offered to spearhead an army of his pals who want to get into the fighting in Palestine." The Bergson Group took out newspaper ads, one of which featured Barney Ross's photograph and a message from the champion:

> There is no such thing as a *former* fighter. We must all continue the fight.

On March 29, in the Bergson Group's New York offices, Ross was photographed signing the rolls for the George Washington Legion, a prospective Jewish-American armed

Ross signing the roll for the George Washington Legion,
a prospective band of Jewish-American war veterans
eager to fight for an independent Jewish state.

force patterned on the famed Abraham Lincoln Brigade of
the Spanish Civil War. Barney was joined by the legion's
British-Jewish organizer, Major Samuel Weiser, who had
been on the staff of Field Marshal Bernard Montgomery in
the war. Within weeks, Ross said he had signed up more than
2,000 volunteers, many of whom were Jewish-American veterans. But the State Department announced that "Barney
Ross . . . probably will be denied a passport to fight for the
Jews in Palestine. That policy would apply to all Americans
recruited for military service in Palestine." In April, he traveled to Washington and met with various United States sen-
ators and congressmen. In a press conference held in the
office of Representative Andrew L. Somers, the Brooklyn
congressman, Ross told reporters:

In the past two weeks, thousands of American veterans have indicated that they are ready to go to Palestine and back up the Hebrew fight. I'm here in Washington to express to Congress the desire of all who have joined the George Washington Legion to get over there fast.

We don't want to be tangled in red tape. When the Flying Tigers went to help China and the Eagle Squadron flew to England there were no obstacles put in their way; and now that Americans want to back up Hebrew freedom, we expect to get the same sort of backing. . . . The men are ready and we hope Congress will open the door so that a division of American volunteers can get to Palestine and make a beachhead for freedom and democracy there.

For Barney, whose own ascent as a prizefighter paralleled the emergence of the Jewish state, it seems natural not only that he would lend his fame to the cause of Zionist freedom, but that this would be perfectly in keeping with American values.

3

The Bergson Group had also made contingency plans to get around the inevitable red tape, developing a variety of extralegal methods with which to smuggle men and matériel into the now-partitioned Palestinian territory. In

Hollywood, Ben Hecht had begun fund-raising among members of the Jewish underworld, addressing a fund-raising party organized by the mobster (and former featherweight boxer) Mickey Cohen. In *A Child of the Century* he tells us of the motley gathering he addressed at Slapsie Maxie's café. "A thousand strangers, some with battered faces, some in society rig, came to the event. . . . I addressed a thousand bookies, ex-prizefighters, gamblers, jockeys, touts and all sorts of lawless and semi-lawless characters; and their womenfolk."

We have no record of Barney Ross being in attendance at Slapsie Maxie's that night—Hecht would likely have mentioned it if he had—but there's evidence that he participated in similar fund-raisers. An unpublished monograph left behind by a member of the Bergson Group recounts that a group of St. Louis Jewish gangsters associated with Cohen agreed to hold a fund-raising dinner for the American League for a Free Palestine, on the condition that the league provide Barney Ross as the keynote speaker. "In their eyes, the former boxer was the living symbol of Jewish toughness," Rafael Medoff has written. "League officials later estimated that thanks to Ross, the event brought in more than $100,000 for the cause of Jewish statehood."

I had long heard stories that Barney Ross had called on some of his old underworld connections in order to run guns for the Irgun. If so, it was a dangerous game; in 1948, a pair of men named Joseph Untermeyer and Isaiah Warsaw had been charged by the New York police with having smuggled guns to the Jewish underground secreted in shipments of clothing. Gangsters like Meyer Lansky are known to have coordinated shipments of armaments to the Jewish underground from the New York docks and, in at least one incident, to have sabotaged a shipment of munitions bound to the Arab fighters in Palestine. During one of my interviews with George Rasof in Niles, I asked him if the stories of his brother as gunrunner were apocryphal. "It's not a myth," George told me. "But I didn't know the truth until I saw it myself."

By November 1947, Barney had taken a new desk job as secretary-treasurer in charge of labor relations for Milton Blackstone's Eureka Shipbuilding Company, and as George recalled, "That's how some of that stuff got in [to Israel].

"I used to go to New York quite a lot for my jewelry business. I'd stay with him in his apartment in the Hampshire House on Central Park South. He left a message once that he wouldn't be back till the following day and I was alone in the apartment and for some reason—God knows why—I started to get a little nosy. There was a big closet, and when I opened it, there was a tarp—a sheet of canvas all rolled up. I pried a little bit and I saw some of these guns in there. Rifles. Machine guns. Heavy weapons. When I saw him that night, I said, 'Barn, what the hell are you mixed up in? You could get yourself hurt.' He says, 'Yunk, don't ask me about that shit.' "

PART EIGHT

1

By his late forties Barney Ross had become a kind of elder statesman of the fight world, described by *The New York Times* as a "small round man with gray hair, chain-smoking cigarettes and softly talking of the years when boxing was more important and its heroes were hungrier." He was inducted into the Boxing Hall of Fame in 1956 (and into the International Boxing Hall of Fame in 1990). He worked occasionally as a referee, making ringside appearances when friend Sugar Ray Robinson fought Jake La Motta at the Garden, throwing posed punches at his friend Rocky Marciano in front of the Barney Ross cottage at Grossinger's.

By now, Milton Blackstone was managing the career of Eddie Fisher, the young Philadelphia-born singer who married Elizabeth Taylor and whose reputation had been made by numerous appearances on *The Eddie Cantor Radio Show*. Barney Ross began to travel the country as Fisher's right-hand man. Some accounts describe him as little more than a glorified bodyguard, chaperoning Eddie Fisher and Elizabeth Taylor to parties and nightclubs, though his official job was as a vaguely defined public-relations executive.

Meanwhile, as he traveled the United States with Fisher,

Ross with his friend, heavyweight champion
Rocky Marciano, and Marciano's fur-clad wife.

he began to make a personal crusade to educate the public
about the reality of drug addiction. He spared none of the
ugly truth of his own descent. His friend Milton Gross wor-
ried about revealing the unsavory details of Ross's $500-a-
week habit: " 'I don't want to write this about you, Barney,'
I said. 'It will shame you.' 'So shame me,' Barney said. 'Tell
it all because maybe it will help somebody else not get into
the spot I was. If I can keep one kid from going on the stuff,
it would be worth it.' " He lectured without fee at hundreds
of civic and service organizations, went to tough inner-city
schools on the West Side of Chicago and in the Bronx, speak-
ing heart-to-heart with sixteen-year-olds who had the
bruises of hypodermic needles on their arms.

"I beat the habit because I wanted to," he told a group of

recovering teenage addicts in New York, "because it was that or the end. You can beat it too if you really want to. . . . They say there's no such thing as a fully cured addict, but that's not true. I'm cured—and I'm not alone."

In September 1955, a Senate investigating subcommittee chaired by Senator Price Daniel, Democrat of Texas, held hearings on narcotics in the United States, and Barney Ross was called to Washington as an expert witness. Waiting his turn to testify, he became incensed when a well-known medical authority started to cite the grim statistics that had been coming out of places like Lexington: that sooner or later almost all heroin addicts, even those treated by the reduction method in U.S. Public Health Service facilities, relapse into heroin use. Ross leapt to his feet and disrupted the hearing: "Here's one fellow who didn't go back and who'll never go back." His shouting caused an uproar in the hearing.

On September 23, when it came time for him to give his sworn testimony before the Senate subcommittee, Ross remained impassioned, according to the *New York Times* account of the proceedings:

> Smugglers and all peddlers except addicts in the business to obtain drugs for their own use "should be hung immediately," according to Mr. Ross, who was light-weight and welterweight boxing champion in the mid-nineteen-thirties. . . . He often pounded the table and raised his voice in telling how he became a morphine user to relieve the pain of battle wounds received as a

Marine on Guadalcanal and conquered the habit after
120 agonizing days as a voluntary patient in the Public
[Health] Service Hospital at Lexington, Ky. On
Guadalcanal, he testified, sick bay attendants were
sometimes so busy that patients gave shots to themselves. At Lexington when dosages were reduced he
went through the "contortions of hell," he said.

According to George Orwell, "autobiography is only to
be trusted when it reveals something disgraceful." Barney
Ross spared little of his own disgrace in *No Man Stands Alone*,
published in 1957. He staked out a position that today may
sound reasonable but was, in fact, hugely controversial at
the time: to decriminalize narcotics and view addiction as a
medical rather than a criminal-justice problem:

> The addict himself should be treated as a sick man,
> because that's what he is. Putting him in jail doesn't do
> anybody any good. He should be sent for the cure, and
> his case should be followed up to see if he can stick to
> the cure. If the doctors become certain that he can't—
> and for the old-timers, particularly, we know there is
> no hope—then, in my opinion, we should treat him the
> way the English do, namely give him the dope he needs
> through a government clinic. . . .
> The only sensible, practical way to kill an accursed
> racket like this is first to treat the racketeers a lot
> rougher, and second, and most important, take all the
> profit out of it. When addicts get free injections at clin-
> ics, they won't be paying customers for the pushers

anymore. And if their treatment is carefully supervised, we'll be doing the best we can for those who are hopeless cases, and also the best we can for society.

In his private life he did more than moralize. For a time, he adopted a Bronx street kid named Charlie who'd become a petty thief and stickup man to support his $125-a-week heroin habit. Father Fred Gehring witnessed the tough treatment Ross practiced. "The boy tearfully insisted that he would do 'anything' to kick the habit. I expected Barney to react with sympathy. Instead, he tore into the youngster with a merciless tongue-lashing. 'Why were you so hard on him?' I asked later. 'Once you become an addict you become a con man,' Barney explained. 'The addict can give you all kinds of tearful excuses and glib promises. Only an ex-addict understands this.' "

The Barney Ross of these years resembles some kind of smashed-nose guardian angel, rushing to take charge of young addicts and veterans, even when he didn't have the financial wherewithal to do so. A news story of the late 1950s describes him showing up at criminal court in Lower Manhattan to post $500 bond for a "36-year-old homeless former paratrooper" named Edward Cleveland who was arrested when the police found him carrying prescription pills in a paper bag. On another occasion, when he heard about an old blind Medal of Honor winner of World War I who was being evicted from his hotel room because of his inability to pay $100 back rent, he paid the debt, proudly marching the old veteran back inside the hotel. He told Father Gehring that he'd borrowed the money from "a guy in the meat business." When an ex-fighter named Frankie Ryff fell down an elevator shaft and became a paraplegic, Barney took him into his apartment, and borrowed more money to pay the medical bills. "The guy's in trouble—you gotta help," he said.

2

He remained true to the code of Chicago's West Side; loyalty to old friends trumped everything, trumped negative headlines, trumped personal shame. On November 24, 1963, when Jack Ruby burst through the crowd of reporters and cops in the Dallas Police Station to fatally shoot Lee Harvey Oswald, he dragged the long murky world of the West Side's Jewish bookmakers, hit men, and hoodlums into the light. Teams of FBI special agents fanned out across the country, interviewing everyone who had known Jacob "Sparky" Rubenstein in his younger years, anyone who might crack the enigma of Jack Ruby.

Had Sparky really been the Outfit's representative in Dallas? Had he been run out of Chicago in 1947 by Lenny Patrick and Davey Yaras, the two mobsters reputed, though never proven, to have been the gunmen who murdered Benjamin "Zookie the Bookie" Zuckerman, the West Side's gambling boss? Yaras, interviewed by the FBI in Joe Pierce's restaurant on Division Street in December 1963, admitted knowing Sparky but asserted that he was "positively on his own and not Outfit-connected." Lenny Patrick, who by the 1960s had

Jack Ruby, killer of Lee Harvey Oswald, poses with three of the
women from his burlesque club in Dallas. (© *Bettman*/CORBIS)

risen to running much of the Outfit's gambling operations
on the far North Side, appeared in sworn testimony before
the Senate's subcommittee on assassinations in 1978 and was
far more voluble than most mobsters of similar rank. He
didn't once plead the Fifth Amendment, said he didn't need
a lawyer to act as an interlocutor, and offered this on Jack
Ruby: "I haven't seen him in years, but he was not a 'wise
guy,' if you know what I mean."

Alongside the names of such infamous Chicago gangsters and bookmakers, the volumes of the *Warren Commission Report* are peppered with references to Barney Ross. Hyman Rubenstein, Ruby's Warsaw-born older brother, testified that Jack had "hung around Barney Ross all his life. He liked Barney Ross. Everybody liked Barney Ross." Asked if he was also a follower of Barney Ross, Hyman Rubenstein shrugged. "Naturally, when you live on the West Side you have got to be a follower."

Barney Ross was interviewed in the FBI's New York office twice: on November 25, 1963, and then again on June 4, 1964. He freely admitted his friendship with Ruby, told how Ruby used to be present at every one of his prizefights, both amateur and professional, often traveling out of town to attend. He said that it was possible that Ruby had met Al Capone when Ross was fighting out of the Kid Howard Gym in Chicago, and that he "might have run innocuous errands for Capone." He also, somewhat farcically, tried to claim that Ruby was generally "well-behaved" and never a troublemaker; this despite the official record, duly noted by the commission: "On June 6, 1922, at the age of eleven, Ruby had been referred to the Institute for Juvenile Research by the Jewish Social Service Bureau. The reason for the referral was 'truancy and incorrigible at home.' "

Ross told the FBI that "he did not know of any criminal activities ever engaged in by Jack Ruby, and he pointed out that among the group that he and Ruby associated with, none of them had ever carried a knife, gun or other dangerous weapon." Yet he surely must have been aware that Jack

Ruby had been arrested by the Dallas Police Department eight times between 1949 and 1963, though never convicted of a crime. The arrests included "carrying a concealed weapon, disturbing the peace, and simple assault." Ruby himself had chalked it up to his upbringing on those same streets that had spawned boxers like Barney Ross, Jackie Fields, Kingfish Levinsky . . . also: Samuel "Nails" Morton, Jake "Greasy Thumb" Guzik, Lenny Patrick, and Dave Yaras: "You learn in the ghetto," Ruby said, "to be a jungle-walker."

When Ruby went on trial, in November 1964, facing the death penalty in the state of Texas, Barney Ross appeared as a character witness for the defense, arriving in the court-room with Ruby's attorney and wearing a narrow diagonally striped tie, a stony expression, and black wraparound sunglasses. He testified after a Yale psychologist, Dr. Roy Shafer—who said that Ruby was likely in a "blacked-out rage" when he shot Lee Harvey Oswald and didn't know what he was doing—and a twenty-one-year-old Dallas strip-tease dancer named Patricia Ann Kohs who worked profes-sionally as "Penny Dollar." The *Chicago Tribune* reported on the famous ex-champion's testimony:

> Ross, 53, said he and Ruby were part of a group of about 10 or 12 teen-agers who palled together nearly 40 years [ago] on Chicago's west side. Ross told the court:
> "We used to have problems with [Ruby]. He was what is known as a good sport and a good handicapper. He was really an authority on handicapping. When we'd

look to make a nickel or a dime wager, he'd scream and go into a tantrum and say, 'Don't bet on this team, bet on the other.'

"He'd almost turn purple and walk away. If fans booed a team he liked, he'd get up and holler and scream and walk away.

"He'd let steam off. He'd be a day or two away from our group and we'd miss him. He just walked away without saying good-by. He was, I'd say, a pretty moody person.

"In arguments about sports, if we didn't see eye to eye with him, he'd get into a frenzy. He'd scream at us—violently. . . . We'd say, 'What's wrong, Jack? Take it easy. Cool down.' "

In its trial coverage, *The New York Times* explained that Barney was wearing his wraparound sunglasses while on the witness stand owing to the fact that his right eye had been injured in his brutal 1935 fight with the Filipino welterweight Ceferino Garcia.

The blow knocked him to the canvas. But he got up and fought several rounds in a dazed condition and eventually won the fight on points. The defense hoped [Mr. Ross] would be able to testify that Ruby, who was sitting ringside during the fight, had fainted when Mr. Ross hit the canvas. But the prosecution successfully blocked the evidence as hearsay.

Indeed, Barney's testimony (and that of all the diverse defense expert witnesses) did little to help Sparky Rubenstein, who was sentenced to death—though that sentence was later commuted to life in prison. He would die of cancer in a prison hospital, two weeks before his old friend Barney Ross succumbed to the same disease. After his court appearance, Barney Ross appeared before television reporters, muttering something about Sparky being "too tough" to control.

3

The end was excruciating and slow, so unlike that of his idol Benny Leonard, who died a most dramatic public death inside a prize ring. On April 18, 1947, eleven days after his fifty-first birthday, while refereeing a match in New York's St. Nicholas Arena, Leonard suffered a massive coronary and had to be carried from the ring on a stretcher. "Something has happened," the ringside announcer said in the radio broadcast. "Benny Leonard has collapsed in the ring." The Ghetto Wizard of the Lower East Side was pronounced dead in the dressing room.

In the spring of 1966, following extensive dental work, Barney Ross began to experience an inexplicable pain in his jaw. A dentist noticed an abnormal growth on the roof of his mouth. Ross checked himself into St. Albans Hospital on Long Island, where he was diagnosed with cancer. The malignancy quickly spread from his palate to his throat.

George Rasof once told me how his brother arrived in Chicago to give him the news that he was dying. "The girl at work told me my brother was on the phone. I said, 'Jesus, Barney, what's wrong with you? You're talking like you got a mouthful of shit.' He had already had all his teeth removed and his mouth was packed with cotton. 'Yunk,' he says, 'call Min [George's wife], tell her you're gonna have dinner with me. Meet me at the Singapore at six o'clock.' Now you realize my brother was never on time in his life. You can't count on your hands the number of times he had to run down the ramp to the plane or the concourse to the train.

"At six o'clock the traffic in the Loop was murder and I got to the Singapore maybe ten minutes late. He was already standing out front on Rush Street, looking at his watch. 'Jesus Christ! Yunk, you're not a kid anymore, you're a businessman. You gotta learn to be on time!' I says, 'You sonofabitch. You've never been on time in your life. I'm late *once* and you're gonna give me hell about it?' We went inside and ordered some drinks. I heard Barney telling the waiter to bring him a martini. I stared at him, and he made a *shhhh!* with his mouth, I already knew that the prognosis was bad. I knew it must be terminal—that it wouldn't make any difference if he continued to drink or smoke."

He insisted on spending his dying days in Chicago. He was an outpatient at the Veterans Research Hospital on the Near North Side, undergoing nearly two months of cobalt treatments. He was in constant pain, and his lips and jaw ballooned so grotesquely that he was scarcely recognizable. He continued to chain-smoke, from the moment he woke up until the moment he fell asleep. His friend Ira Colitz paid for Barney and Cathy to live in his large apartment at 1000 Lake Shore Drive so that the dying fighter could look out at Lake Michigan and "the dark lines of the city he loved so well." He kept up a brave front for reporters. "I'm still in there swinging and I'll lick this thing too," he rasped to one sports columnist. Many of the old-timers who'd watched his courageous ring battles said that they almost believed him.

4

In those final months, Ross was, again, very much the disciple of Daniel Mendoza. Mendoza had, according to boxing historian Ken Blady, "cultivated extravagant pursuits and a carefree lifestyle. He lacked business acumen, and was never able to stay at one thing for very long. His debts began to pile up; so much so that the former toast of the town was confined within the rules of the King's Bench."

In 1935, in the blush of youth and seemingly endless championship purses, Barney Ross had once told a Chicago journalist how he was carefully "socking away" his money. "I have seen and heard of many fighters winding up broke and that's one thing I'm trying to avoid. . . . The way things shape up just now everything is very rosy and I hope that the day never comes when they will have to run a benefit for me, as they have done for many of the fighters."

But now he too found himself depending on the charity of friends. "Where have I been for thirty years?" he rasped to a reporter in 1966 from his sickbed. "Have I been sleeping or something? Here I am, maybe ready to cash in, and there's not enough dough for the kid [Cathy]." The fighting fraternity rallied in a series of testimonial dinners. The first tribute was staged in late November in the Sunnyside Garden in Queens, fittingly one of the last neighborhood fight clubs in New York. BARNEY ROSS FINDS HIS FRIENDS DON'T FORGET, read the headline spanning the top of *The New York Times* sports section, and the story describes how Barney, from his bed on Lake Shore Drive, listened to the tributes over the phone, and even managed some banter with Izzy Jannazzo, whom Ross had beaten for the championship in late November 1936. The aged featherweights Willie Pep and Sandy Sandler staged a mock reenactment of one of their classic bouts, and the ringside seats were filled by Floyd Patterson, Jimmy Braddock, Tommy Loughran, Paul Berlenbach, Mickey Walker, Rocky Graziano, Jake La Motta, Carlos Ortiz, Dick Tiger, Joey Archer, Petey Scalzo, Billy Graham, Frankie Ryff, Bruce Flowers, and Tony DeMarco. Max Schmeling sent a $100 contribution in an airmail letter from Germany. Frank Sinatra and Jackie Gleason each donated $1,000. Onstage, Father Fred Gehring, who had led a contingent of Barney's friends from Jack Dempsey's restaurant in Midtown, accepted a check for $13,000. Jimmy Cannon, who had been in the press row to cover some of Ross's epic championship fights, leaves us a vivid description of the night:

> The boxers came in and the bangers, the clowns and
> the dogs, some champions and the cuties, the hookers

and the jabbers and the murderers who could take you out with a shot. It worked for Barney when he could use his legs and stick with his left hand. The ropes sheltered him from the world. It was all wrong once he walked out of the dressing room. The dice took it and the horses . . . he bet baseball and he never welshed. He picked up as many tabs as he could lift and he was hooked on junk and he would even stand for a touch when he wasn't holding. . . . I imagine this was a benefit Wednesday night. But I saw it another way. They were just paying Barney Ross what he was owed. The whole world is in debt to a man like this. He didn't have to win a title to be a champion.

On December 12, 1966, a similar "Salute to Barney Ross" was staged in Chicago's Loop Theater. Barney was far too ill to attend, but he sent Cathy to "tell everyone at the party to have a good time." Five hundred friends and well-wishers, including Floyd Patterson and Muhammad Ali and twenty Marines with Purple Hearts from the Vietnam War, gathered to watch the old films of Barney Ross fighting Billy Petrolle, Ceferino Garcia, and Jimmy McLarnin. The crowd was silent at the newsreel footage of the relentless battering he had taken in those final rounds against Henry Armstrong in 1938. The almost superhuman stoicism of that fight seemed the most apt tribute of the night. Cathy was presented with a check for $25,000, and though more fund-raising events were already being planned, Barney's family issued a statement asking for the discontinuance of benefits. "The family now feels that all of Barney's needs have been met and that his friends have contributed enough," Ben Rasof said in late December.

5

In Barney's last ambulance ride to Veterans Research Hospital, he reportedly turned to Ira Colitz and asked, "Is this the last round I've got?" Colitz assured him that it wasn't. "There was a slow negative twist of Barney's head and the softest of chuckles came from his twisted lips. 'Don't forget to give my business to Hershey,' he said, referring to his friend Hershel Weinstein, owner of one of Chicago's oldest funeral chapels. He asked to be allowed to die at home, so they took him back to Colitz's Gold Coast apartment where, a few minutes after 10 a.m. on January 17, 1967, at the age of fifty-seven, Ross died.

Ira Colitz kept his word, and the funeral was held at the Original Weinstein & Sons Chapel on the North Side. Barney Ross was buried in Jewish Rosemont Cemetery, where Father Fred Gehring added the Catholic prayer "Our Father" to those of the officiating rabbis. "I'm only repaying my organist for that favor left over from Christmas Eve," Gehring said.

"A student of the Talmud who turned to prizefighting," read *The New York Times* obituary, "Barney Ross was regarded as one of the toughest champions. Outside of the ring, moreover, his heroism on Guadalcanal and his victory over a

Barney David Ross: "soft-spoken and happy-go-lucky outside the ring, but inside it a furious machine, completely devoid of fear."

narcotics habit brought him further recognition as a man who had never been knocked out and had never quit."

Milton Gross offered a more personal elegy in his column. "He was born Barnet Rasofsky, but he should have been named Job. . . . He went all the way against cancer and those of us who loved this kindly, crazy wastrel of a man were almost glad. Barney loved life. He loved the night hours and people around him. He loved to gamble. He loved to play the piano. He loved to throw money away. Nobody deserved happiness more, but how many wars must a man fight in and out of the ring before peace can come to him?"

PART NINE

1

Philip Roth—born March 19, 1933, three days before Barney Ross beat Billy Petrolle on his epic campaign to the lightweight title—writes in his memoir *Patrimony* about an afternoon spent with his father during which they discuss the bygone days of Jewish prizefighting. It's the late 1980s, and the novelist, frightened by the physical and mental deterioration in his father, Herman, a retired insurance salesman from Newark, arrives at his father's house in Elizabeth hoping to get him to sign a living will. But seeing Herman's badly depressed state, he finds it too hard to bring up his intended subject and instead turns the conversation to Jewish boxers. In a bookstore on Upper Broadway he stumbled upon a copy of Ken Blady's obscure oral history, *The Jewish Boxers' Hall of Fame*, and though he'd long ago lost interest in the sport, he knows that his father still greatly enjoys watching prizefights on television.

"I asked him how many of the old-time Jewish fighters he thought he could name," Philip Roth writes. Herman Roth easily summons Abe Attell, Battling Levinsky, Benny Leonard, Ruby Goldstein, and Lew Tendler, the tough left-handed Philadelphian who'd fought Benny Leonard and later opened a popular steakhouse.

"They were terrific characters. They were poor boys, just like the colored, that made the grade in boxing. Most of them wasted their money, they died poor men. The only one I think made money was Tendler. I remember the era very vividly of Tendler, Attell, and Leonard. Barney Ross. He was a heulluva fighter. I saw him fight in Newark. There was Bummy Davis—he was a Jew. There was Slapsie Maxie Rosenbloom. Sure, I remember them. . . . They'd put two guys in the ring, an Italian and a Jew, an Irishman and a Jew, and they fought like they meant it, they fought to hurt. There was always a certain amount of hatred in it. Trying to show who was superior."

The elder Roth briefly muses on the immigrant conditions that produced the bumper crop of Jewish pugilists: "You know how it was: these kids grew up, they had a tough life, the slums, no money, and they always had an adversary. The Christian religion was an adversary. They fought two battles. They fought because they were fighters, and they fought because they were Jews."

2

The neighborhoods that produced these memorable fighters—the dense, working-class Jewish enclaves of New York, Chicago, Newark, and Philadelphia—have largely vanished. Recently, I drove my rented Grand Am looking for the surviving shards of Barney Ross's Chicago. The original Maxwell Street market no longer exists; it was razed decades ago so that the city could build the Ryan Expressway. On West Roosevelt Road, the new breed of gangsters stand in bandannas and Nike Air Force One sneakers, bass-heavy hip-hop rattling the tinted windows of tricked-out SUVs. The Anshei Lubavitch synagogue where the Rasofskys worshiped still stands, though it has been a Baptist church for years.

To drive through Chicago today, one might think that the world of Barney Ross's youth had been some kind of mirage, a riotous dream of Jewish gunmen and bookmakers, fighting furriers and smashed-nose boxers slipping through the taut ropes in the Marigold Gardens, or holding court over martinis in the Chez Paree. The generation of Jewish boxers disappeared so precipitously after Barney Ross's reign that, by the time my mother and father were seniors in North Side Chicago high schools in 1947 and 1948, there were scarcely any Jewish professional fighters of note in the United States. To me, this sudden tear in the lineage stretching back to Mendoza's reign is like the extinction-level events my father, a petroleum geologist, used to speak about in the "K/T," or Cretaceous-Tertiary boundary. There are practically no tales of second-generation Jewish fighters, just as few Jews followed their gangster fathers into the criminal milieu. Sports historian George Eisen has accounted for it by observing that, unlike many other ethnic groups, "Jews have always viewed sports participation as a means for achieving something else—gaining social status or scholarships to universities, or going into business—not an end in itself."

I drove for several days through Chicago and its northern suburbs, stopping in numerous restaurants and bars, mentioning my research into the life story of Barney Ross. In this great blue-collar city where he was once one of the most famous of sportsmen, he is scarcely remembered, certainly not held among the pantheon of the city's athletic legends like Walter Payton, Dick Butkus, Bobby Hull, Michael Jordan. Informed boxing fans, of course, know the truth: not too many years ago, a reader wrote to the *Sun-Times* asking an expert for his ranking of the greatest boxers to come out of Chicago; Barney Ross was still ranked at the top, followed by his close friend, another fighter in the Pian-Winch stable, the tough Polish-American middleweight Tony Zale.

Ross's grave site in Rosemont Cemetery is today rarely visited. I recently knelt on the springy turf, swept away the dried grass clippings with my fingers, left a jagged pebble as a memento on the edge of his headstone. The next morning I sat with his brother George, picking at slices of cantaloupe and halved bagels in the sun-splashed dining hall of the Golf Mill Estates. Aside from the staff, I seemed to be the only person under eighty in this sunroom. One of the men at our table was a contemporary of Barney's from the West Side; he'd also seen combat in World War II, although he'd been shooting at the Wehrmacht and the Waffen S.S., not soldiers of the Imperial Japanese Army. This wheelchair-bound ninety-three-year-old in a neatly pressed plaid shirt leaned over to tell me a story about Barney's famous big-heartedness, a wonderful yarn about how the champion had left a back entrance of the Chicago Stadium unlocked so a bunch of the guys from Roosevelt Road could stream in without paying. Those were tough Depression times, and not everyone had the money to buy tickets. He quavered in joy at the memory: that was the night Beryl had first beaten Babyface—Scourge of the Fighting Sons of Israel.

George Rasof listened patiently, nodding, seeming to enjoy the retelling of the story. He didn't have to worry about offending this old West Sider, who as it turned out was almost wholly deaf.

"He doesn't know what the hell he's talking about," George said at last. "He's *farblondzhet*. All three fights with Jimmy McLarnin took place in New York. The first two were in the Madison Square Garden Bowl and the rubber match at the Polo Grounds. But listen, at this point, let him *think* what he wants to think."

3

Returning to my own West Side, the lower Hell's Kitchen neighborhood in Manhattan where I lived with my wife and infant daughter, I found more of Barney Ross's legacy than I'd ever imagined. A small second-floor boxing club had opened up down the block from my apartment on 9th Avenue, replacing a decrepit pool hall that I'd never had the courage to set foot in. I joined the boxing gym and began to train with Ilan Benshoshan, one of the owners, a twenty-nine-year-old Sephardic Jew from Tel Aviv. He was a swarthy, powerfully built kickboxer—he'd won trophies in Israel in the fast-growing sport of traditional Thai boxing, or Muay Thai, fighting out of Tel Aviv's Megiro Gym. He told me that in his rough South Tel Aviv neighborhood, Sh'chunat Hatikvah, and the neighboring section called Tel Kabir, many kids from impoverished Sephardic backgrounds either became criminals or proficient boxers, and the Israeli gangsters, especially the Alperon crime family— then embroiled in a series of murderous bomb battles for control of the gambling and loansharking rackets in Tel Aviv—often sent emissaries to the boxing academies looking to recruit new muscle. Ilan referred to one infamous Alperon enforcer as "Chaim Thailandi"—Muay Thai is known in Hebrew as *Igruv Thailandi*—and he and his friends reverently described the exploits of their teachers, the champion fighters Shuki Ron and Udi Salame, the way I had heard ultra-orthodox Brooklyn teenagers discussing their rebbes.

Late at night, before the gym closed at 11 p.m., a few of his friends from the old neighborhood came to wrap their fists and train with demonic fury; I would take my nose out of my sheaves of 1930s *Ring* magazine clippings and my dog-eared copy of Barney Ross's *Fundamentals of Boxing* to watch the burly young Israeli army veterans sparring and grunting. Ilan instinctively reverted to Hebrew when calling out his instructions, barking, "*Magal!*" for a hook, "*Smol!*" for a left jab, "*Tashar!*" for a straight punch. His best friend, Avi Sardas, a shaved-headed, thick-necked Sephardic Jew who always wore a pair of silver hoop earrings—I took to teasingly calling him Mr. Clean—unleashed a savage left hook on the heavy bag that echoed like a gunshot, and for a fleeting moment, in a yellow-roped ring above 9th Avenue, I got a glimpse of a new living crop of Daniel Mendoza's disciples.

One Saturday night I walked a dozen blocks north through Hell's Kitchen, past homeless men camped in piles of rancid clothes near the Port Authority Bus Terminal—one hollow-eyed man asked me for fifty cents so he could buy a pack of chocolate cupcakes—then wandered into the Actor's Temple on West 47th Street. Founded in 1917, Congregation Ezrath Israel is a small grey-brick synagogue, its front doors painted a sky-blue gloss. It nearly closed permanently several years ago, but a devoted core of several dozen younger members has kept the *shul* alive. I hadn't remembered that it was Purim, and at the entrance of the wood-paneled sanctuary a woman was handing out small plastic cups of inexpensive cognac. "Have a schnapps," she said (the word my Bialystok-born grandfather, Willie, would have used), urging me to get drunk tonight, too drunk to be able to tell the name of the hero, Mordecai, from the name of Haman, the villain. The whirring noisemakers, tambourines, and maracas were drowning out every mention of wicked Haman, and several small girls were running down the aisle in brightly colored Mardi Gras masks. I sat in the creaking wooden pews, reading along to the Purim *megillah*, surrounded by the stained-glass windows and plaques dedicated to the memories of showbusiness luminaries such as Jack Benny, George Jessel, Sophie Tucker, and Joe E. Lewis who had worshiped here a few generations back.

After the reading of the *megillah*, the congregation moved

to a basement, where the celebration continued over platters of hamantashen and bottles of hard liquor. On another *yahrzeit* wall of vaudevillian names, I looked up to see two small bronze memorial plaques, one for Barney Ross and one for his murdered father, Isidore Rasofsky. I poured myself a full glass of vodka—the little prizefighter's favorite drink—and silently repeated the phrase Jimmy Cannon had penned in his 1966 column. "He didn't have to win a title to be a champion."

Barney mentions toward the end of his memoir, *No Man Stands Alone*, that his whole family would gather from around the country on Purim, one of his favorite Jewish festivals. The holiday, a minor one, seemed an odd but a fitting choice for a man who wore so many masks in his own life: the boxer, the soldier, the junkie, the Jew, the bighearted Samaritan, the self-destructive street tough. Of course, the Purim story itself ends with a fantasy of Jewish power: Mordecai avenges his people by ordering the slaughter of the Persian plotters.* The call to violence has troubled Jewish commentators for centuries. Barney Ross was everything the Diaspora tradition had warned Jews not to become, but a fulfillment as well of its secret fantasy.

*Megillat Esther 8:11: Mordecai sends out instructions, sealed with the royal signet, that "the king was permitting the Jews in every city to assemble to defend themselves, and to destroy, kill and annihilate the armed force of any people or province attacking 'them, their women and their children . . . the thirteenth day of the twelfth month, which is Adar.' "

AFTERWORD

1

Unlike Philip Roth, my own father never shared with me an encyclopedic knowledge of Jewish prizefighters, though he could lay claim to having bought a necktie from Kingfish Levinsky. Growing up in western Canada, I had often heard him mention this peculiar detail from his Chicago youth, usually coupled with a more comprehensible— at least to my young ears—account about how my Uncle Bernie and he had chased down Cubs' pitcher Dizzy Dean's autograph, or how they'd listened to the radio broadcast of Sid Luckman quarterbacking the Bears to their 73-to-0 shellacking of the Redskins in the 1940 NFL championship.

The transaction with the Kingfish took place in the Loop, sometime in the later years of World War II, where my Warsaw-born grandfather Lou, a mink-cutter and member of the International Fur and Leather Workers Union, had landed my father an after-school job removing nails from mink pelts attached to plywood boards. Nailing pelts was a necessary step in stretching the furs before they were taken over by the surgical fingers of professional mink cutters like my grandfather. One afternoon the small shop echoed with a Falstaffian bellowing—the fur workers turned to see a hulking six-footer with a smashed nose and cauliflower ears carrying a valise. Several sets of spectacled eyes rolled at the return of the King. Hershel Krakow had long been one of the Loop's more notorious characters, and most boxing aficionados regarded him as a clown for the way he had flailed around the squared circle like a hooked marlin in his Comiskey Park fight with Joe Louis, suffering three knockdowns in the first round. Some experts said the King hadn't even been knocked out—he'd fainted at the sight of another of the Brown Bomber's straight rights—though the consensus among reporters was that he'd sat on the lower rope in a neutral corner and through "chalk-like lips" begged referee Norman McGarrity to stop the fight. In 1943, according to court papers, his wife, "Roxanne the Fan Dancer," had referred to the Kingfish as an "alleged fighter" when she sued him for divorce. ("Those who do not agree with King Levinsky that King Levinsky is a prizefighter were joined yesterday by his wife," reads the *Tribune* account of the divorce proceeding.) A decade after his retirement the now-punchy King would make his daily circuit in the Loop, selling ties from his battered valise. He would slip the tie around the neck of prospective customers, cajoling, chuckling, undercutting his own prices, which were never more than "a deuce, four bucks, or even a fin," although Al Capone once—according to Kingfish's later recollection to author Ira Berkow—dropped fifty bucks for a cravat from the King Levinsky collection. My father, then fourteen or fifteen, watched in amazement and, gathering with all the other fur workers, politely picked out a printed silk tie that

he knew he would never wear. The King was a tireless salesman and didn't shut his case until he'd put a tie in the hands
of every man in the shop.

Those Jewish furriers didn't look much like fighters. In
the group photographs I have from the 1920s and '30s—my
grandfather, a short pensive man in wire-rimmed glasses,
served as a delegate to the National Furriers Conference in
1934—they all seem to have the softly rubbed features and
high foreheads of physics professors, poets, or concert
pianists. Yet some, like my grandfather's close friend Lew
Goldstein, had actually been boxers. In their time the Jewish
furriers developed a fierce reputation, having battled, and
beaten, the infamous thugs of Louis "Lepke" Buchalter's
mob when the gangsters tried to muscle their way into control of the union in New York and Chicago. Irving Howe,
certainly no apologist for their far-left politics, writes in
World of Our Fathers: "The Communist furriers developed a
psychology rare in modern Jewish history and previously
unknown in the immigrant milieu: the psychology of shock
troops, a sort of paramilitary vanguard handy with knives,
belts, pipes No one in the garment center was tougher than
they, no one claimed to be." Such mettle was a sharp con-
trast to Kingfish Levinsky's buffoonish physicality, this
"vanguard" composed of shop stewards like my Grandpa
Lou, who read Tolstoy and *Das Kapital* and sang Yiddish lul-
labies with his uncle, Chaim. My father told me that he once
in fact saw the *shtarker*—the unofficial enforcer in my grandfather's local—an immigrant worker who, like my grandfather, stood five feet five. He was sipping a glass of hot tea,

sitting hunch-shouldered in a nondescript Loop restaurant, reading a labor column in the Yiddish *Freiheit*.

2

For years I've ruminated on these long-vanished images of Jewish toughness—the 250-pound former contender barking over his gaudy collection of neckties; that tiny tea-sipping union leg-breaker. Such picaresque figures were largely absent from my upbringing in western Canada, and Chicago, from my child's perspective, became a city of 3 a.m. delicatessen ghosts, gruff Yiddish-speaking men in boxy gray suits, punctuating their profane opinions with soggy-tipped White Owl cigars.

From 1940 through the late 1960s, my mother's family was in the restaurant business. They owned a popular twenty-four-hour delicatessen called S&L—for my grandfather, Willie (Velvel) Smith, and my uncle, Abe Levy—located on Kedzie and Lawrence avenues in Albany Park. By the time I was old enough to visit Chicago, the family had sold the "store" and all that remained were a few black-and-white photographs, receipts for corned beef sandwiches and 10-cent chocolate phosphates, and Uncle Abe's stories of obsessive gamblers, cops on the take, and young draftees bound for combat in Europe and the Pacific.

They were the characters from Barney Ross's world, and my uncle—born one year after Barney, in 1910, on Manhattan's Lower East Side—could summon them like smoke-shrouded genies in his den in West Rogers Park. He told me about Jewish gangland characters who had dressed in police uniforms—procured by a certain Captain Shapiro at the Albany Park precinct—in order to go pick up a visiting Nazi official who was coming to Chicago to address the Bund; the Jewish police "escort" met the Nazi at the train station, drove him to a secluded street, beat him half-dead with pipes and baseball bats and sent him back to Germany. He told me about one pathetic gambler who won a small fortune with the bookies across the street from the restaurant, wooed and wed the sexiest woman in Albany Park, and promptly lost everything—his gleaming car, furnished apartment, and glamorous wife—when his lucky streak deserted him.

By the mid-seventies, when I was a boy, my uncle was out of the restaurant business and had returned to his original career—for which he'd been trained in the 1920s in Staten Island—as a pharmacist. His den was filled with mementos from his stint as a pharmacist in the United States Army during the second world war, his staff sergeant's stripes, Asiatic-Pacific campaign ribbon with four bronze campaign stars denoting service in New Guinea, Leyte, Luzon, and Hollandia, and the Philippine Liberation Ribbon. There were photos of Abe and his buddies posed in the jungle of Corregidor, my uncle holding a bazooka and a friend hanging from the barrel of the largest artillery gun I'd ever seen.

At age 34 and the father of two small children, my uncle had been too old for the draft, but after Pearl Harbor the delicatessen began offering going-away breakfasts for the enlisted men and draftees. And after months of handing these neighborhood teenagers a farewell carton of cigarettes, my uncle felt he had to enlist. Like Barney, his reasons weren't entirely patriotic; many decades later he told me that in his thirties, he'd become seriously depressed, lost in a fog of aimlessness and despair, and going off to war seemed like the best possible solution. He told the local draft board that if they didn't move his number up, S&L would stop having the going-away breakfasts.

He was assigned to the U.S. Army's 745th Medical Hospital Ship Platoon (Separate) and his strange adventures in the South Pacific always provided the most fantastic stories. Souvenir hunting one day in British New Guinea, he and his friend Harry Bourie wandered into a village of "fuzzy-wuzzies"—naked warriors with hair bleached a greenish yellow from lime juice, teeth filed to razor-sharp points. Their chief, wearing a headdress decorated with the red circle from a package of Lucky Strike cigarettes, asked them to stay for dinner. It took a passing Jeep of Australian soldiers to warn them of their peril: "Stupid Yanks! Look at their filed teeth. They're bloody cannibals and you're the next meal."

It hardly mattered to me whether the stories were 100 percent true—*emmes a Torah* as my friends and I used to say at the Peretz *shul*—they filled my ears with a magical cadence, like Jim Hawkins hearing the drunken braying of "Fifteen men on a dead man's chest" from a buccaneer campfire. On each of the converted luxury liners of the Matson Line—the *Lurline*, *Monterey*, and *Matsonia*—my uncle had saved a slip of paper, the size of a playing card, his bright blue eyes glinting with mischief as he told me that the god Neptune had issued them to ensure safe passage:

DOMAIN OF NEPTUNUS REX

To all Sailors, Mermaids, Sea Serpents, Whales, Sharks and all other Living Things of the Sea, greetings: Know ye that in the month of August 1944, in Latitude 0000, there appeared in Our Royal Domain the *s.s.* LURLINE. Be it known by all Sailors, Marines, Landlubbers, and others that:

S/Sgt. Abe Levy

While aboard this vessel was found worthy to be numbered as One of Our Trusty Shellbacks. I hereby command all the subjects to show due honor and respect whenever he may enter Our Realm. Disobey this under penalty of Our Royal Displeasure.

By the time I began working on this book, my uncle had died at age 91, and was buried next to my grandparents in Westlawn Cemetery, not far from the headstone of Jack Ruby. I listened often to the tape recordings I made of his storytelling, seeking the flavor of voices from the Chez Paree and the Barney Ross Cocktail Lounge. One of his wartime snapshots has haunted me: it shows my uncle standing in a white government-issue T-shirt inside his bottle-lined pharmacy aboard the *Matsonia*, the closet-sized room from which he would dispense prescriptions of atabrine, quinine, and morphine to injured and ill servicemen like Barney David Ross.

3

Of the books I've used in research, Barney's own memoir, co-authored by Martin Abramson, *No Man Stands Alone* (New York: J. B. Lippincott Company, 1957), is at once the most fascinating, frustrating, and unreliable. Decades before NBA forward Charles Barkley and baseball pitcher David Wells made similar claims, Barney Ross was the first sports celebrity to say he had been misquoted in his own autobiography. He was cooperative with his coauthor, but as Irwin Ross, Barney's nephew, told me, Marty Abramson complained that he could never pin the restless prizefighter down for more than a few minutes at a time to pick his brain. Consequently, the memoir is chock-full of inconsistencies and errors, beginning with the very first sentence, "It happened at seven-thirty in the morning, Thursday, December 13, 1924." The murder of Ross's father had, in fact, occurred on that date in 1923.

Nonetheless, *No Man Stands Alone* is a useful resource for certain of Barney's emotional recollections; wherever possible, I checked those sentiments with the man who knew him best, his last surviving brother, George Rasof.

Barney Ross's long-out-of-print prizefighting primer, *Fundamentals of Boxing* (Chicago: Ziff-Davis Publishing Company, 1942), was a revealing window into the fighter's training regimen and boxing philosophy, and his essay "For Our Kind of World," originally published in *Esquire* in 1943 and collected in the volume *Fighting for America: An Account of Jewish Men in the Armed Forces—from Pearl Harbor to the Italian Campaign* (New York: The Jewish Welfare Board, 1944), was in some respects the most immediate account of his heroism on Guadalcanal.

For the texture of the bygone world of Chicago's Near West Side ghetto, I turned to Ira Berkow's comprehensive *Maxwell Street: Survival in a Bazaar* (Garden City, N.Y.: Doubleday & Company, 1977); particularly helpful were his firsthand interviews of boxers Jackie Fields and King Levinsky, and his biographical sketches of Jake Guzik, Jack Ruby, and Earl Ruby.

I have quoted from Michael Gold's novel *Jews Without Money* (New York: Horace Liveright, Inc., 1930), Ernest Hemingway's *The Sun Also Rises* (New York: Scribner's, 1926), Philip Roth's *The Facts* (New York: Farrar, Strauss & Giroux, 1988) and *Patrimony* (New York: Simon & Schuster, 1991), Saul Bellow's *The Adventures of Augie March* (New York: Modern Library, 1965), Ben Hecht's *A Child of the Century* (New York: Simon & Schuster, 1954), David Remnick's *King of the World* (New York: Random House, 1998), A. J. Liebling's collections *The Sweet Science* (New York: Viking, 1956) and *A Neutral Corner* (New York: North Point Press, 1990), John Keegan's *The Second World War* (New York: Viking, 1990), Irving Howe's *World of Our Fathers* (Simon & Schuster, 1976), Isaac Zaar's *Rescue and Liberation: America's Part in the Birth of Israel* (New York: Bloch Publishing Company, 1954), Harold U. Ribalow's *The Jew in American Sport*

(New York: Bloch Publishing Company, 1948), and Robert Jay Nash's *World Encyclopedia of Organized Crime* (New York: Da Capo Press, 1993).

Other works I drew upon were *When Boxing Was a Jewish Sport* (Praeger, 1997) by Allen Bodner, *Jazz Age Jews* (Princeton, N.J.: Princeton University Press, 2001) by Michael Alexander, *Capone's Chicago* (Lakeville, Minn.: Northstar Maschek Books, 1987) by Ray Cowdery, *Man Against the Mob* (New York: Ivy Books, 1989) by William E. Roemer, Jr., *This Is Guadalcanal* (New York: William Morrow, 1998) by Douglas Keeney and William S. Butler, *The Encyclopedia of World Boxing Champions*, *The Boxing Register*, 3rd edition by Alexander Skutt and James Roberts (2002), and *The Encyclopedia of Boxing* by Gilbert Odd (1989).

For historical information about Daniel Mendoza I turned to a strangely fascinating book—the one which Philip Roth bought on upper Broadway to bring to his ailing father—*The Jewish Boxers' Hall of Fame* by Ken Blady (New York: Shapolsky Publishers Inc., 1988). Also: *The Fireside Book of Boxing*, edited by W. C. Heinz (New York: Simon & Schuster, 1961).

Among the nonliterary sources I have drawn on are the films *Body and Soul*, directed by Robert Rossen (1946); *Monkey on My Back*, directed by Andre de Toth (1957); and *Requiem for a Heavyweight*, in which Barney Ross has a small cameo role as himself.

Kurt J. Noltimier, a boxing archivist who maintains a library of vintage fight films in Edina, Minnesota, provided me with rare footage of Barney Ross fighting Tony Canzoneri, Jimmy McLarnin, and Henry Armstrong.

The research library at the International Boxing Hall of Fame in Canastota, New York, provided me with copies of Nat Fleischer's *The Ring*, often called "The Bible of Boxing," which widely covered Ross's championship years from 1933, when he first fought Tony Canzoneri for the lightweight belt, through 1938, when he lost his world's welterweight belt to the indefatigable Henry Armstrong.

In the Microforms Reading Room of the New York Public Library, I drew upon hundreds of articles in the *Chicago Tribune*, *Chicago Times*, *New York Times*, New York *Daily News*, *New York Post*, and several now-defunct newspapers. I'm grateful to the library staff for specially ordering from the University of Chicago library the microfilm of the December 1923 *Chicago Daily News* containing a news account of the murder of Barney's father.

I have quoted from two essays by George Eisen, "Jewish History and the Ideology of Modern Sport: Approaches and Interpretations" from *Journal of Sport History*, volume 25, number 3, and "Jews and Sport: A Century of Retrospect" from *Journal of Sport History*, volume 26, number 2.

I have also made reference to the Rev. Frederic P. Gehring's short memoir of Barney Ross, "The Most Unforgettable Character I've Met," from *Reader's Digest*, March 1968; Milton Gross's "Barney Ross, Wednesday's Child," from *Boxing Illustrated*, June 1993; Dan Daniel's "Greatest Moments of Courageous Barney Ross," from the April 1967 issue of *The Ring*; and Red Smith's "The Life of Triple-Crown Winner Barney Ross: One Big Battle," from the August 1981 issue of *The Ring*.

4

I owe an immense debt to George Rasof, who spent countless hours with me, answering questions, clarifying names and dates, opening both his home and his heart to me. As I sat in his living room in Niles, flipping through the stacks of wire-service photographs, each image would pull forth a new memory, joke, or yarn. I found a picture of Barney in San Francisco with his nattily attired friend, the one time heavyweight champion Max Baer. Baer had boxed with the Star of David on his silk trunks and was hugely popular with Jewish fans, especially after beating German heavyweight Max Schmeling in 1933. Though Baer's father was half-Jewish and his mother Scotch Irish, he sometimes professed to being a practicing Jew. George remembered a photograph that had appeared on the front page of a Yiddish paper showing Maxie kneeling inside a Catholic church; Ma Rasofsky wagged her finger at him. "*Du darf zach shemen,*" she said. Max shrugged at Barney; he couldn't understand rudimentary Yiddish. "What'd she say?" " 'You should be ashamed,' " Barney told him, laughing.

I was fortunate to have tape-recorded dozens of such conversations with "Yunk," knowing that with his passing, an entire world of memories from the heyday of Jewish prizefighting would be lost. I had hoped that the diminutive former Golden Glover, who told me he felt conflicted about living most of his life in his famous brother's shadow, would live to see his words in print. But after a long and painful illness, George died in November 2004 at age 87. He too now lies buried in Westlawn Cemetery on Chicago's North Side.

I'm grateful to Erwin Ross, Barney's nephew, born a week after the murder of Itchik Rasofsky—a retired accountant, he fondly recalled taking the streetcar every weekday to my grandparents' delicatessen for lunch—and to Alvin Rasof, Barney's first cousin, who shared many memories via phone and mail.

My friend and editor Jonathan Rosen provided a constant source of encouragement and inspiration. I'm also grateful to the entire Nextbook publishing staff for their help in seeing this book come to fruition. Thank you to Dan Frank at Schocken Books for his sharp editorial eye. And as ever, thanks to my agent Sloan Harris.

For their advice, encouragement, and inspiration, I'd like to thank my parents, Marcia and Jack Century; the boxing writer Jason Probst; and Ilan Benshoshan, Avi Sardas, and Eli Waizman, the crew of Sephardic fighters from Tel Aviv who showed me firsthand that the era of Jewish ring craft isn't merely a thing of memory.

CHRONOLOGY

project to spread Greek culture among the
Jews; Jews engage in nude Greek athletic
contests, even attempting to reverse their
circumcisions.

167–164 BCE A family of priests from the Galilee leads a
revolt against the Hellenistic regime in
Jerusalem. Led by Judah the Maccabee
(the Hammer), they win religious freedom for
Judea and restore the Temple.

37 BCE King Herod begins erecting sports stadiums
around Judea, establishes Olympics every
five years and brings athletes from around the
world to compete in them.

70 CE Destruction of the Temple in Jerusalem by
Roman army.

132 Bar Kochba leads a Jewish army in revolt
against Roman rule.

135 Emperor Hadrian defeats the Jewish rebellion,
executes leaders including the sages, some of
whom are tortured in the Coliseum.

c. 250 Simon ben Lakish, a Jewish gladiator, changes
profession to rabbi; he is later known as Resh
Lakish.

740 The army of the Khazars, a central Asian
kingdom whose elite class converted to

Judaism, halt the advance of Muslim armies into Europe

C.1384 In Weisenfeld, Germany, Jews, who are forbidden from participating in medieval tournaments—essentially paramilitary training for knights—are for a brief period permitted to engage in their own version of these tournaments.

C. 1487 Tournaments in Rome designate a day for Jewish competition; Jews distinguish themselves particularly in running. These exercises continue through the seventeenth century, sometimes taking on the flavor of mock tournaments for the amusement of gentiles.

1555 In his great code of Jewish law, the *Shulchan Arukh*, sephardic Rabbi Joseph Caro forbids ball playing on the Sabbath. His Ashkenazic counterpart, Rabbi Moses Isserles, in his gloss on the *Shulkhan Arukh*, permits it.

1792 Daniel Mendoza, billed as the "Light of Israel" and "Mendoza the Jew," is sixteenth champion of the London Prize Ring, wins patronage of the Prince of Wales. Coins are struck in his honor, and he is the first Jew known to have conversed with King George III.

1881–1882 First Jewish self-defense groups of the modern era organize in the face of pogroms in Russia

1896   Six Jewish athletes win thirteen
       medals at first modern Olympics,
       in Athens.

1898   Max Nordau, at the Second Zionist
       Congress in Basel, calls for muscular
       Judaism.

1901   Bantamweight Harry Harris is first
       Jew to win world championship under
       Marquis of Queensberry rules.

1903   Devastating pogroms in Kishinev and
       around Russia, inspire Bialik's "In the
       City of Slaughter" and renewed
       interest in Jewish self-defense.

DECEMBER 23, 1909   Dov Ber Rasofsky born to Sarah and
       Itchik Rasofsky on the Lower East
       Side.

1911   Rasofskys move to Chicago's Maxwell
       Street ghetto, where they own a small
       grocery.

1917   Nails Morton, local Chicago gangster
       and defender of Jews, arrested for
       beating Polish gang members to death.

1917   A Bronx-born tailor's son, Jacob
       Golomb, begins manufacturing
       boxing headgear for Jack Dempsey.
       Golomb's company, Everlast, founded

as a swimwear maker in 1910, expands to making boxing gloves and trunks and today remains the most famous maker of boxing equipment.

1919   The "Black Sox" scandal rocks the sporting world; Jewish gambling kingpin Arnold Rothstein is accused—though never convicted—of fixing the World Series, using former featherweight boxing champion Abe Attel as his messenger.

c. 1920   Meyer Lansky and his pal Benny (a.k.a. Bugsy) Siegel, two tough Jewish kids from the Lower East Side, begin their climb to the top of organized crime, involved not only in racketeering but also in smuggling liquor during Prohibition, legal and illegal gambling, and numerous other mob activities.

1922   Nat Fleischer founds *The Ring* magazine, the most authoritative publication of boxing.

JULY 1923   Two Jewish boxers, Benny Leonard and Lew Tendler, battle for world lightweight championship.

DECEMBER 13, 1923   Itchik Rasofsky, father of Dov Ber, killed in robbery.

1924   Jackie Fields, né Jacob Finkelstein, wins featherweight gold medal at Paris Olympic Games.

1926   Rasofsky, now known as Barney Ross, begins fighting as an amateur, wins Chicago Golden Gloves tournament.

MAY 1, 1926   Hakoah-Vienna, an all-Jewish soccer team touring the United States, plays before 46,000 fans at New York's Polo Grounds, setting an American soccer attendance record that would stand until 1977.

MARCH 27, 1929   Fighting in the New York-Chicago Intercity Golden Gloves championship, held in Madison Square Garden, Ross beats Al Santora to win the 126-pound title.

SEPTEMBER 1, 1929   Ross wins first professional fight, in LA against Raymond Lugo.

MARCH 20, 1931   Ross beats Jackie Davis in Chicago.

1932   Jimmy McLarnin knocks out Benny Leonard, who returns to retirement.

OCTOBER 21, 1932   Ross beats Battling Battalino at Chicago Stadium.

JANUARY 1933 Ross succeeds in getting Georgie, the last of his siblings, out of the orphanage.

JUNE 23, 1933 Ross, in split decision, beats Tony Canzoneri for junior welterweight title.

SEPTEMBER 12, 1933 Ross-Canzoneri rematch goes to Ross.

SEPTEMBER 15–17, 1933 *The Romance of a People* staged in the Polo Grounds, in response to rise of Nazism.

MAY 17, 1934 A pro-Nazi rally held by the German-American Bund attracts over 20,000 Hitler supporters to Madison Square Garden.

MAY 28, 1934 Ross beats Jimmy McLarnin for welterweight title.

JUNE 4, 1934 Ross returns to Chicago with hero's welcome.

SEPTEMBER 17, 1934 Second Ross-McLarnin fight goes to McLarnin in split decision; fight date chosen so as not to conflict with High Holy Days.

Barney Ross

SEPTEMBER 19, 1934   Hank Greenberg, the Detroit Tigers'
first baseman and a legendary
home-run hitter, refuses to play in
the World Series on Yom Kippur.

MAY 28, 1935   Third Ross-McLarnin fight goes to
Ross.

1935   Ross's brother, George Rasof, wins
flyweight novice division in Golden
Gloves .

1936   Ten Jewish athletes win medals at the
Berlin Olympics.

DECEMBER 5, 1937   Ross marries Pearl Siegel.

MAY 31, 1938   Ross loses world championship to
Henry Armstrong, retires from
boxing.

NOVEMBER 9, 1938   *Kristallnacht*, a Nazi-sponsored
pogrom, devastates Jewish
communities of Germany and Austria.

1940   Quarterback Sid Luckman takes
Chicago Bears to NFL Championship.

1940   Ross opens cocktail lounge in Chicago.

LATE WINTER 1942   Ross and Siegel separate.

FEBRUARY 3, 1942   Ross enlists in the Marines.

SPRING 1942 Marries Cathy Howlett in San Diego at the end of basic training.

NOVEMBER 4, 1942 Ross's company lands at Guadalcanal.

NOVEMBER 19, 1942 Ross's patrol attacked by Japanese soldiers; he fights them off overnight, defending several injured comrades and sustaining severe injuries himself, wins Silver Star for his actions.

FEBRUARY 9, 1943 U.S. forces in control of Guadalcanal.

FEBRUARY 26, 1943 Ross arrives in San Diego; after convalescence in military hospital he embarks on morale-raising tour of the country despite the morphine addiction he developed while in the hospital.

MARCH 9, 1943 The Bergson Group, an American militant Zionist organization, stages pageant "We Will Never Die" in Madison Square Garden, among the earliest public exposure of the atrocities taking place in Europe.

1943 Ross publishes *The Fundamentals of Boxing.*

APRIL 11, 1944 Ross receives honorable discharge from Marine Corps, descends further into addiction.

1946 Cathy separates from him; granted provisional divorce.

1946 Ross checks himself into U.S. Public Health Service Hospital in Lexington, KY, to treat addiction to morphine formed when recovering from army wounds.

JANUARY 1947 Ross released from detox.

APRIL 18, 1947 Death of Benny Leonard.

MAY 1947 Ross sponsors goodwill tour of United States for Haifa soccer team.

NOVEMBER 1947 Ross takes job with ship-building company, engages in arms running for Jewish army in Palestine.

1947 John Garfield, born Jacob Julius Garfinkle, stars in *Body and Soul*, a film clearly based on Ross's boxing and military career.

JANUARY 1948 Mickey Marcus, an American Army Colonel, arrives in Palestine to serve as military advisor to the army of the future State of Israel.

MARCH 29, 1948 Ross signs up for Jewish-American armed forces to fight in Palestine; official force never authorized by Congress.

MAY 14, 1948 State of Israel established.

SEPTEMBER 23, 1955 Ross testifies before Senate
subcommittee on narcotics addiction.

1957 Ross publishes his autobiography, *No
Man Stands Alone.*

1957 Release of film based on Barney's life,
Monkey on My Back.

NOVEMBER 24, 1963 Jack Ruby arrested for killing Lee
Harvey Oswald. Ross interviewed by
FBI regarding Ruby's possible Mafia
connections in their Chicago youth.

1965 Sandy Koufax refuses to pitch in the
World Series on Yom Kippur.

1966 Ross diagnosed with oral cancer.

JANUARY 18, 1967 Ross dies in Chicago.

SEPTEMBER 5, 1972 Eleven Israeli Olympians are taken
hostage by Palestinian terrorists at
the Munich Olympics; all are killed.

Mark Spitz wins a record seven gold
medals in swimming at the Games, is
escorted out of Munich under high
security after the terrorist strike.

2001 Dimitry Salita, a Russian Jew living

in New York, wins Golden Gloves. An Orthodox Jew, Salita refuses to fight on Sabbath or holidays.

AUGUST 25, 2004 Gal Friedman wins Israel's first Olympic gold medal, in windsurfing.

APPENDIX

1929

Sep 1	Ramon Lugo	Los Angeles	W 6
Sep 14	Joe Borola	Los Angeles	W 6
Oct 12	Joe Borola	Los Angeles	W 6
Oct 21	Virgil Tobin	San Francisco	KO 2
Nov 19	Joey Barth	Chicago	W 5
Dec 5	Al DeRose	Chicago	W 6

1930

Jan 10	Louis New	Chicago	W 6
Jan 24	Johnny Andrews	Chicago	W 4
Feb 22	Jiro Kumagai	San Francisco	W 4

Mar 17	Jackie Davis	St. Louis	ND 4
Apr 8	Eddie Bojack	Cleveland	KO 2
Apr 21	Carlos Garcia	Chicago	L 6
Apr 25	Mickey Genaro	Chicago	W 6
Jul 1	Eddie Koppy	Detroit	W 8
Aug 7	Luis Navaro Perez	Chicago	KO 1
Sep 19	Young Terry	Chicago	D 8
Oct 14	Sammy Binder	Chicago	TKO 2
Nov 6	Petey Mack	Chicago	KO 1
Nov 21	Harry Dublinsky	Chicago	D 8

1931

Jan 14	Harry Falegano	Chicago	W 8
Feb 20	Young Terry	Chicago	W 10
Mar 20	Jackie Davis	Chicago	W 6
Mar 27	Roger Bernard	Chicago	L 8
Apr 8	Midget Mike O'Dowd	Moline, IL	W 8
Apr 24	Lud Abella	Chicago	TKO 2
May 1	Jackie Dugan	Moline, IL	KO 8
May 13	Mickie Billy Shaw	Chicago	W 10
Jul 15	Babe Ruth	Benton Harbor, MI	KO 4
Jul 30	Jimmy Alvarado	Detroit	W 8
Oct 2	Glen Camp	Chicago	W 10
Nov 4	Lou Jallos	Chicago	W 8
Nov 13	Young Terry	Moline, IL	W 8
Nov 18	Jimmy Lundy	Kansas City	W 8

1932

Feb 8	Mickey O'Neill	Milwaukee	W 6
Feb 18	Billy Gladstone	Chicago	W 6
Mar 2	Nick Ellenwood	Muncie, IN	W 10
Apr 5	Frankie Hugues	Indianapolis	W 10
May 20	Dick Sisk	Chicago	TKO 6
Jul 28	Henry Perlick	Chicago	KO 3
Aug 26	Ray Miller	Chicago	W 10
Sep 15	Frankie Petrolle	Chicago	KO 2
Oct 21	Bat Battalino	Chicago	W 10
Nov 11	Goldie Hess	Chicago	W 10
Nov 26	Johnny Farr	Milwaukee	W 10

1933

Jan 20	Johnny Datto	Pittsburgh	KO 2
Feb 22	Tommy Grogan	Chicago	W 10
Mar 22	Billy Petrolle	Chicago	W 10
Mar 26	Tony Canzoneri	Chicago	W 10
	(*Wins World Lightweight and World Jr. Welterweight Titles*)		
May 4	Joe Ghnouly	St. Louis	W 10
Jul 26	Johnny Farr	Kansas City	TKO 6
Sep 12	Tony Canzoneri	New York	W 15
	(*Retains World Lightweight and World Jr. Welterweight Titles*)		

| Nov 17 | Sammy Fuller | Chicago | W 10 |

(Retains World Jr. Welterweight Title)

1934

| Jan 24 | Billy Petrolle | New York | W 10 |
| Feb 7 | Pete Nebo | Kansas City | W 12 |

(Retains World Jr. Welterweight Title)

| Mar 5 | Frankie Klick | San Francisco | D 10 |

(Retains World Jr. Welterweight Title)

Mar 14	Kid Moroo	Oakland	W 10
Mar 27	Bobby Pacho	Los Angeles	W 10
May 28	Jimmy McLarnin	New York	W 15

(Wins World Welterweight Title)

| Sep 17 | Jimmy McLarnin | New York | L 15 |

(Loses World Welterweight Title)

| Dec 10 | Bobby Pacho | Cleveland | W 12 |

(Retains World Jr. Welterweight Title)

1935

| Jan 28 | Frankie Klick | Miami | W 10 |

(Retains World Jr. Welterweight Title)

| Apr 9 | Henry Woods | Seattle | W 12 |

(Retains World Jr. Welterweight Title)

| Apr | Abandons Lightweight and Jr. Welterweight Titles |

May 28	Jimmy McLarnin	New York	W 15
	(Regains World Welterweight Title)		
Sep 6	Baby Joe Gans	Portland, OR	TKO 2
Sep 13	Ceferino Garcia	San Francisco	W 10
Nov 29	Ceferino Garcia	Chicago	W 10

1936

Jan 27	Lou Halper	Philadelphia	TKO 8
Mar 11	Gordon Wallace	Vancouver, BC	W 10
May 1	Chuck Woods	Louisville	KO 5
Jun 10	Laddie Tonelli	Milwaukee	KO 5
Jun 22	Morrie Sherman	Omaha, NE	KO 2
Jul 22	Phil Furr	Washington, DC	W 10
Nov 27	Izzy Jannazzo	New York	W 15
	(Retains World Welterweight Title)		

1937

Jan 29	Al Manfredo	Detroit	W 10
Jun 17	Chuck Woods	Indianapolis	KO 4
Jun 27	Jackie Burke	New Orleans	KO 5
Aug 19	Al Manfredo	Des Moines, IA	ND 10
Sep 23	Ceferino Garcia	New York	W 15
	(Retains World Welterweight Title)		

1938

Apr 4	Henry Schaft	Minneapolis	TKO 4
Apr 25	Bobby Venner	Des Moines, IA	TKO 7
May 31	Henry Armstrong	Long Island City, NY	L 15

(Loses World Welterweight Title)

ABOUT THE AUTHOR

Douglas Century is the author of *Street Kingdom* and, with Rick Cowan, of the *New York Times* best seller and Edgar Award-finalist *Takedown: The Fall of the Last Mafia Empire*. Publications he has written for include *The New York Times*, *Details*, *Rolling Stone*, and *The Guardian*. He lives in New York.